Lonely planet

POCKET

BOSTON

TOP EXPERIENCES · LOCAL LIFE

T0018148

MARA VORHEES

Contents

Public Garden (p64)
F11PHOTO/SHUTTERSTOCK ©

Explore Boston 31

Worth a Trip

Survival Guide 147

COVID-19

We have re-checked every business in this book before publication to ensure that it is still open after the COVID-19 outbreak. However, the economic and social impacts of COVID-19 will continue to be felt long after the outbreak has been contained, and many businesses, services and events referenced in this guide may experience ongoing restrictions. Some businesses may be temporarily closed, have changed their opening hours and services, or require bookings; some unfortunately could have closed permanently. We suggest you check with venues before visiting for the latest information.

Top Experiences

JULIEN HAUTCOEUR/SHUTTERSTOCK ©

Wander the Stacks at Boston Public Library

A treasure trove of beautiful works. **p106**

Marvel at the Murals in Trinity Chruch

Architect Henry Hobson Richardson's crowning achievement.
p108

Soak Up the Atmosphere at Fenway Park

America's most beloved ballpark.
p126

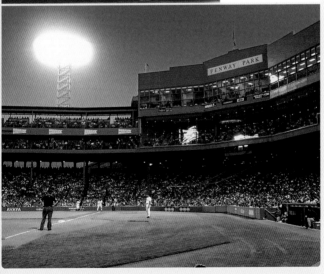

Unleash Your Culture Vulture at the MFA
Eclectic, encyclopedic art museum. **p122**

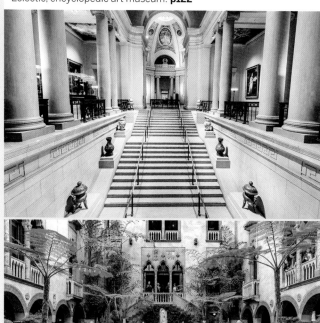

Admire the Art at Isabella Stewart Gardner Museum
An art connoisseur's quirky collection. **p124**

Take a Breather in the Public Garden
An oasis of greenery and serenity. **p64**

Step Back in Time in Harvard Yard
The historic heart of Harvard University. **p134**

Savor Science at MIT
Cutting-edge science and innovative art. **p136**

Experience the New at the ICA
A pioneer of Boston's contemporary art scene. **p76**

Hop Around Boston Harbor Islands

Take in the views and the sea air. **p88**

People Watch on Boston Common

Boston's historic green centerpiece. **p60**

Dining Out

The Boston area is the home of the first Thanksgiving and of bountiful autumnal harvests. It's also America's seafood capital. In this era of creative culinary discovery, many Bostonians are reclaiming their roots in one crucial way: through appreciation of local, seasonal and organic products.

Beantown

With a nickname like Beantown, you know that Boston is into food. Culinary historians believe that Native Americans cooked beans with fatty bear meat and molasses in earthenware pots. Early settlers likely adapted this recipe by substituting pork for bear meat, resulting in the famed Boston baked beans. Despite the name, you'll have some trouble finding baked beans on a menu in Boston today.

International Influences

The international influence on Boston cuisine cannot be underestimated. A tight-knit immigrant enclave, the North End is an upholder of old-fashioned Italian American cooking, with ristoranti and *pasticcerie* (bakeries) on every corner. In the 20th century, a new wave of immigrants arrived from South America and Asia, bringing the flavors of Brazil, China, India, Korea and Vietnam.

Seafood

Evolving from its environment, Boston cuisine has always featured plenty of seafood, especially the 'sacred cod,' halibut and various shellfish. Lobster – once so plentiful that it was served to prisoners – is now a recognized delicacy that appears on most local menus. Many restaurants have 'raw bars' where they serve local oysters and clams on the half-shell.

DARRYL BROOKS/SHUTTERSTOCK ©

Best Budget Dining

El Pelon Fish tacos. Cheap. Delicious. (p129)

Eventide Fenway Oysters on the cheap. (p129)

Best Seafood

Saltie Girl Sample the delicacies at this seafood bar. (p115)

Row 34 Eight kinds of oysters, five kinds of fish; seafood galore. (p84)

Best Italian

Pomodoro The most romantic hole-in-the-wall on Hanover St. (p52)

Coppa Enoteca An upscale *enoteca* (wine bar) in the trendy South End. (p100)

Best Asian

Gourmet Dumpling House Often packed, but always worth the wait for soup dumplings. (p99)

Myers + Chang Asian-inspired small plates from local celebrity Joanne Chang. (p100)

Best Brunch

Beehive Listen to jazz and feast on eggs *shakshuka*. (p101)

Paramount An old-fashioned family place where they still call it breakfast. (p69)

West End Johnnies JC's corned-beef hash and eggs plus live reggae music equals happiness. (p55)

Top Tips For Tipping

In restaurants with sit-down service, customers should leave a 15% tip for acceptable service and a 20% tip for good service; tipping at a lower level reflects dissatisfaction with the service.

Bar Open

Despite the city's Puritan roots, Bostonians like to drink. While Boston has its fair share of Irish pubs, it also has a dynamic craft-beer movement, with more and more microbreweries opening; a knowledgeable population of wine drinkers; and a red-hot cocktail scene, thanks to some talented local bartenders. So pick your poison...and drink up!

Where to Drink

Boston's drinking scene is dominated by five categories: dive bars, Irish bars, sports bars and truly hip cocktail bars. Nowadays there are also plenty of beer bars and local breweries, but any of these types might cater to discerning beer drinkers, with local craft brews on tap or a wide selection of imported bottles.

Aside from Dunkin' Donuts on every corner, there are scores of cute cafes and cool coffeehouses, many of which serve dynamite sandwiches and pastries. Many also offer free wi-fi – another inducement to linger.

Where to Dance

The main neighborhood in Boston where the dancing goes down is the Theater District. Boylston St is the main drag, but there are venues all over this groovy 'hood. There are also clubs in Back Bay, Fenway, Cambridge and Downtown.

Best Cocktails

Drink Let the mixologists mix something that suits. (p86)

Yvonne's Scrumptious cocktails get lined up on this gorgeous mahogany bar. (p85)

Ward 8 West End bar serving up the namesake cocktail and many others. (p54)

Best Beer

Trillium Fort Point A beer hall serving a Boston original. (p86)

Bukowski Tavern More kinds of beer than we could count, served with plenty of sass. (p117)

Best Cafes

Thinking Cup Delectable coffee and irresistible pastries – right across from the Boston Common. (p87)

ROMAN BABAKIN/SHUTTERSTOCK ©

Best Sports Bars

Bleacher Bar Big sandwiches and Boston beers, with a view into Fenway Park. (p130)

Caffé Dello Sport Here's how they do sports bars in Italy. (p55)

West End Johnnies Upscale sports bar near the TD Garden. (p55)

Best Views

Lookout Rooftop Bar Fabulous views of the harbor and environs. (p86)

Pier Six Watch the sun drop behind the Boston city skyline. (p39)

Trillium Fort Point Take a peek from the rooftop deck. (p86)

Best LGBTIQ+

Club Café The fun never stops with dinner, dancing, karaoke and gay cabaret. (p116)

Best Dancing

Lansdowne Pub Cover-band dance parties on Friday and Saturday nights. (p131)

Good Life Three bars and two dance floors: take your pick. (p87)

Hitting the Clubs

∘ Expect to pay a cover charge of $10 to $20 at clubs.

∘ Most clubs enforce a dress code.

∘ Check club websites in advance to get on a guest list.

Show Time

Welcome to the Athens of America, a city rich with artistic and cultural offerings. We're talking not only about the world-class symphony orchestra and top-notch theater and dance companies, but also rock clubs, poetry slams and avant-garde performance art. Not to mention the championship sports teams that fans live and die by.

Music

Home to the **Boston Symphony Orchestra** (p131) and the New England Conservatory of Music, Boston boasts some of the country's oldest and most prestigious houses for symphonic experiences.

Boston's modern music scene is centered in the student areas of Cambridge and Allston/Brighton. There's also a thriving jazz scene, starting with the students and faculty of the Berklee College of Music. To figure out who's playing where, take a look at the clubs' websites or listings in *Dig Boston* (www.digboston. com). Most shows are for those aged 21 and over.

Theater

The Theater District is packed with venues showcasing the city's opera, dance and dramatic prowess, while more innovative experimental theaters are in Cambridge and the South End. The Boston Ballet (www. bostonballet.com) performs at the **Boston Opera House** (p87), also in the Theater District. Two opera companies – Boston Lyric Opera (www.blo. org) and Odyssey Opera (www.odysseyopera.org) – perform at venues around town.

Comedy

Boston is a funny place, and we mean funny ha-ha. To cite some famous examples, Conan O'Brien, Jay Leno and Denis Leary are all from Boston. **The Wilbur Theatre** (p102) is Boston's largest comedy venue, but the local talent is normally found at smaller funny outlets all around town.

STEPHAN SCHLACHTER/SHUTTERSTOCK ©

Best Live Rock

Sinclair This venue near Harvard Sq books awesome indie bands. (p145)

House of Blues Where the big names play. (p131)

Best Jazz & Blues

Wally's Café You won't have the blues for long at this legendary club. (p101)

Red Room @ Cafe 939 Not only jazz and blues, but all kinds of experimental and innovative music. (p118)

Beehive Subterranean spot with a 1920s Paris jazz-club vibe. (p101)

Best Theater

American Repertory Theater Racking up Tony awards for its interpretations of classic musicals. (p144)

Huntington Theatre Company Winner of the Tony Award for Outstanding Regional Theatre. (p131)

Boston Center for the Arts Home to a slew of independent theater companies, including the radical Company One. (p101)

Best Comedy

Improv Asylum Dark humor in a dark basement. (p56)

Wilbur Theatre National acts perform here. (p102)

Worth a Trip: Dance Like a Student

Some of Boston's best music clubs are located in Boston's gritty 'student ghetto' west of the center, including **Great Scott** (www.greatscottboston.com), **Brighton Music Hall** (www.crossroadspresents.com) and **Paradise Rock Club** (www.crossroads presents.com).

Treasure Hunt

Boston is known for its intellect and its arts, so it's great for bookstores, art galleries and music shops. The streets are also sprinkled with offbeat boutiques – some carrying vintage treasures and local designers. Besides to-die-for duds, indie shops hawk handmade jewelry and arty, quirky gifts. Fun to browse, even if you don't buy.

Fashion

Fashionistas continue to take their cues from New York, but a few local designers are trying to put Boston on the map à la mode. The styles tend to be relatively down to earth and decidedly wearable compared to what you might see in *Vogue* magazine.

Food & Drink

Some of Boston's best souvenirs are consumables. Stock up on standard New England favorites such as maple syrup, artisanal cheeses and chocolates, and cranberry anything. Browse North End specialty shops for all things Italian, or explore Chinatown for Asian ingredients and medicinal herbs.

Locally Made

Boston's vibrant art scene makes its presence known in local shops, galleries and markets dedicated to arts and crafts. Sometimes quirky and clever, sometimes sophisticated and stylish, these handmade, locally made items are hard to classify, but easy to appreciate.

Best Fashion

Salmagundi Head toppers to fit every style. (p56)

Paridaez A local designer shows off innovative styles for modern busy women. (p70)

Sault New England Cool clothing and unusual gifts from South End style mavens. (p103)

Best Sportswear

Converse at Lovejoy Wharf Iconic sneakers with designs to suit every taste. (p57)

Marathon Sports Buy your sneakers at the Boston Marathon finish line. (p119)

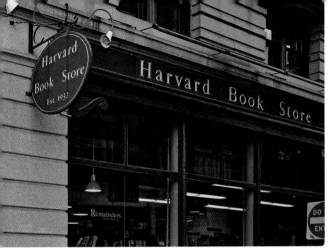

WANGKUN JIA/SHUTTERSTOCK ©

Best Bookstores

Harvard Book Store Excellent bookstore with a jam-packed schedule of lectures and author talks. (pictured; p145)

Brattle Book Shop Treasure trove of used books, with an excellent section on local history. (p86)

Trident Booksellers & Café Long hours, good food and well-stocked shelves. Nothing better. (p118)

Best Food & Drink

Cardullo's Gourmet Shoppe A fabulous selection of specialty food stuffs. (p145)

Boston Public Market Top spot for local delicacies, including nuts, chocolate, beer and more. (p84)

Beacon Hill Chocolates Divine candies in artistic packaging. (p71)

Best Locally Made

SoWa Open Market The city's biggest and best artists' market. (p102)

Cambridge Artists Cooperative Two-level gallery of exquisite, handcrafted pieces. (p145)

Saving on Sales Tax

There is no sales tax in Massachusetts on clothing up to $175 because – get this – it's a necessity! Now, if we could only convince our frugal partner of the *necessity* of those designer jeans...

For Kids

Boston is one giant history museum, the setting for many lively and informative field trips. Cobblestone streets and costume-clad tour guides can bring to life the events that kids read about in history books, while hands-on experimentation and interactive exhibits fuse education and entertainment.

DOMINIONART/SHUTTERSTOCK ©

Best History

USS Constitution & Museum Explore the warship and experience life as a sailor. (p36)

Boston Tea Party Ships & Museum Take part in the historic protest. (pictured above; p80)

Old South Meeting House Scavenger hunts and activity kits reveal the historic building. (p80)

Best Museums

Museum of Science Countless opportunities to combine fun and learning. (p50)

New England Aquarium See eye to eye with thousands of sea species. (p83)

Boston Children's Museum Climbing, constructing and creating, especially for kids aged three to eight. (p82)

Best Adventures

Boston Harbor Islands Swimming, hiking and exploring. (p88)

New England Aquarium Whale Watch Whale sightings are practically guaranteed. (p83)

Public Garden Swan boat rides on the lagoon. (p64)

Best Tours

Boston by Foot Offers the only Freedom Trail tour designed for children. (p22)

Boston Duck Tours Ride the raging waters of the Charles River; quacking loudly is encouraged. (p22)

Travelers with Kids

○ Kids aged 11 and under ride the T for free; older kids pay half-price.

○ Most museums and activities offer reduced rates for children. Art museums are free for kids under 17 years (evenings and weekends only at the MFA).

Museums

JAMES KIRKIKIS/SHUTTERSTOCK ©

*Don't let a rainy day get you down.
Boston is packed with world-class museums that will keep you entertained
and educated...and dry.*

Best Science Museums

New England Aquarium All
the creatures of the sea and
shoreline. (p83)

Museum of Science
Hundreds of exhibits and
experiments to thrill your
inner scientist. (pictured
above; p50)

Best Art Museums

Museum of Fine Arts Boston's premier venue for art,
spanning multiple centuries
and the entire globe. (p122)

**Institute of Contemporary
Art** Sometimes spectacular
and sometimes strange, but
always stimulating. (p76)

**Isabella Stewart Gardner
Museum** An exquisite
Venetian palazzo packed
with art. (p124)

Harvard Art Museums
Three fabulous museums
under one roof (p142)

Best History Museums

**Boston Tea Party Ships
& Museum** An interactive
museum that allows visitors

to participate in revolutionary events. (p80)

Old State House Authentic
artifacts and interesting exhibits, especially focusing on
the Boston Massacre. (p80)

USS Constitution Museum
Learn all about a sailor's life
in 1812 and the history of
the US Navy. (p36)

**John F Kennedy Presiden-
tial Library & Museum**
The legacy of the 35th
President. (p82)

Old South Meeting House
Discover key moments
in Boston history at the
birthplace of the Boston Tea
Party. (p80)

History

For all intents and purposes, Boston is the oldest city in America. And you can hardly walk a step over its cobblestone streets without running into some historic site.

ARCHITECT: I M PEI; MARCIO JOSE BASTOS SILVA/SHUTTERSTOCK ©

Best Historic Pub

Warren Tavern One of the country's oldest taverns, this historic watering hole is named for Dr Joseph Warren, who died in the Battle of Bunker Hill. (p38)

Best Gravesites

King's Chapel Burying Ground John Winthrop, first governor of the Massachusetts Bay Colony. (p81)

Granary Burying Ground Paul Revere, the fearless rider and patriot. (p68)

Mt Auburn Cemetery Henry Wadsworth Longfellow, the poet who retold American history. (p142)

Best Revolutionary History

Freedom Trail The 2.4-mile walking trail includes Boston's most important revolutionary sites. (p22)

Boston Tea Party Ships & Museum This museum includes replicas of the merchant ships that hosted the historic tea party. (p80)

Best Kennedy Family History

John F Kennedy Presidential Library & Museum Learn about JFK's legacy at the official presidential library. (pictured above; p82)

Edward Kennedy Institute for the US Senate Check out the newest Kennedy venue, this one a tribute to JFK's brother. (p82)

Worth a Trip

Four of the nine Kennedy children were born and raised in this modest house in Brookline, now the **John F Kennedy National Historic Site** (www.nps.gov/jofi). JFK was born in the master bedroom in 1917. Take a guided tour.

Spectator Sports

JOSEPH SOHM/SHUTTERSTOCK ©

Boston is fanatical about sports. And why not? The city is home to four professional sports teams – the Bruins, Celtics, Patriots and Red Sox – all of which have won championships in the past two decades.

Baseball

The intensity of baseball fans has only grown since the Boston Red Sox broke its 86-year losing streak and won the 2004 World Series (and three times since). The Red Sox play from April to October at Fenway Park (pictured; p126).

Football

With six Super Bowl victories in the new millennium, the New England Patriots are a football dynasty that is much loved at home but detested in other parts of the country.

They play at **Gillette Stadium**, south of Boston in Foxborough. The season runs from late August to January.

Hockey

Stanley Cup winners in 2011, the Boston Bruins (www. bostonbruins.com) play ice hockey at the TD Garden (p56) from mid-October to mid-April. College hockey is also huge in Boston.

Basketball

The Boston Celtics have won more basketball championships than any other NBA team, most recently in 2008. From October to April, they play at TD Garden (p56).

Best Annual Sporting Events

Boston Marathon (www. baa.org) One of the country's most prestigious marathons takes place on Patriots' Day.

Head of the Charles Regatta (www.hocr.org) The world's largest rowing event takes place on the Charles River in mid-October.

Beanpot Tournament (www.beanpothockey.com) Local college hockey teams compete in February.

Hub on Wheels (www. hubonwheels.com; ⊙ Sep) This citywide bicycle ride starts at City Hall Plaza and offers three routes.

Under the Radar Boston

PAVEL L PHOTO AND VIDEO/SHUTTERSTOCK ©

You don't have to stray too far from the Freedom Trail to lose the crowds in Boston. Away from the city center, you'll discover uncrowded open spaces, unheralded historic sites and unusual museums, as well as vibrant neighborhoods where locals live, work and play.

Neighborhood Vibes

Ride the C-line to Brookline to see the birthplace of John F Kennedy, to lunch at local Jewish delis, or to catch a flick at the art deco **Coolidge Corner Theatre** (290 Harvard St, Brookline, www.coolidge.org; ☎617-734-2500; tickets $9-13). In Jamaica Plain, stately homes overlook a quaint glacial pond, ideal for strolling or sailing. Downtown JP is **Centre St** – that's where you'll find an eclectic assortment of eateries and delightful neighborhood shopping. Across the harbor in **East Boston** (fondly known as 'Eastie') the city's last stretch of undeveloped waterfront offers some of the best views around – and a few new drinking establishments for those in the know.

Offbeat Museums

Collection of Historical Scientific Instruments (1 Oxford St, www.chsi.harvard. edu; ☎617-495-2779; ⏰11am-4pm Sun-Fri) Benjamin Franklin's collection of cool science gadgets.

Mary Baker Eddy Library & Mapparium (pictured above; p112) A spectacular, stained-glass globe that is large enough to walk through.

Larz Anderson Auto Museum (15 Newton St, Brookline, www.larzanderson.org; ☎617-522-6547; ⏰10am-4pm Tue-Sun; admission adult/child $10/5) Dozens of fabulous old automobiles are housed in a handsome carriage house.

Green Spaces

Arnold Arboretum (125 Arborway, www.arboretum.harvard.edu; ☎617-524-1718; ⏰dawn-dusk) An enticing urban oasis, bursting with thousands of species of exotic trees and flowering shrubs.

Franklin Park Five hundred acres of recreational opportunities, including walking trails, playgrounds, ponds and picnic areas.

For Free

Boston can be an expensive city, but it only takes a bit of research to entertain yourself for free. Here are some options for culture vultures and history buffs with empty pockets.

ARCHITECT: RICHARD J SHAW; FELIX
MIZIOZNIKOV/SHUTTERSTOCK ©

Free Tours

Freedom Trail The National Park Service (NPS) offers a free walking tour. (p114)

Black Heritage Trail Another free NPS walking tour that explores the history of African American settlement in Beacon Hill. (p68)

Free Museum Nights

Museum of Fine Arts Free on Wednesday evenings. (p122)

Institute of Contemporary Art Free on Thursday evenings. (p76)

Boston Children's Museum Almost free ($1) on Friday evenings. (p82)

Free Parks & Gardens

Public Garden Stop and smell the roses. (p64)

Rose Kennedy Greenway Walk the labyrinth for free. (p81)

Mt Auburn Cemetery Free garden walks and views from Washington Tower. (p142)

Charles River Esplanade Free strolling. (p112)

Free Art & History

Boston Public Library Free daily guided tours. (p106)

Massachusetts State House Free admission, free tours. (p68)

Charlestown Navy Yard Free tour of the USS *Constitution*. (p36)

Bunker Hill Monument Free view from the top. (p35)

JFK National Historic Site Free visit to the birthplace of the 35th president. (p20)

Free University Tours

Massachusetts Institute of Technology Free campus tours. (p136)

Harvard University Free campus tours. (p135)

Free Entertainment

Hatch Memorial Shell The place for free summertime entertainment. (pictured above; p112)

Shakespeare on the Common Free outdoor theater. (p63)

Four Perfect Days

Day 1

JOE DANIEL PRICE/GETTY IMAGES ©

Spend your first day following the Freedom Trail. It starts at the Boston Common and continues through downtown. Highlights include the **Granary Burying Ground** (p68), the **Old South Meeting House** (p80), the **Old State House** (p80) and **Faneuil Hall** (p82).

The Freedom Trail continues into the North End, where you can visit the historic **Paul Revere House** (p50), **Old North Church** (p50) and **Copp's Hill Burying Ground** (p50). Cross the Charlestown Bridge to see the **Charlestown Navy Yard** (pictured; p36) and the **Bunker Hill Monument** (p35).

Move on to the exquisite Liberty Hotel, former site of the Charles St Jail, and have a drink in the former drunk tank, now the cocktail bar, **Alibi** (p54).

Day 2

CO LEONG/SHUTTERSTOCK ©

Spend the morning admiring Boston's most architecturally significant collection of buildings, clustered around Copley Sq: the **Boston Public Library** (p106), **Trinity Church** (pictured; p108) and the **John Hancock Tower** (p109).

Your afternoon is reserved for one of Boston's magnificent art museums. Choose between the excellent, encyclopedic **Museum of Fine Arts** (p122) or the small but no less extraordinary **Isabella Stewart Gardner Museum** (p124).

There is music in the air this evening. It might be emanating from the acoustically perfect Symphony Hall, where you can hear the **Boston Symphony Orchestra** (p131). For a rowdier experience, catch a baseball game at **Fenway Park** (p126).

Day 3

Rent a bicycle and cycle along the **Charles River** (pictured; p144). Depending where you start, the route passes both **Harvard University** (p134) and **MIT** (p136) campuses. Ambitious riders can return along the Charles River Esplanade and end near Harvard Sq.

While away an afternoon in Harvard Sq, browsing the bookstores, cruising the cafes and catching a free campus tour. If you're in the mood for a museum, the university offers several excellent **options** (p142).

See whatever brilliant or bizarre production is playing at the **American Repertory Theater** (p144). Alternatively, catch a band at **Club Passim** (p144) or the **Sinclair** (p145), or just patronize the buskers in Harvard Sq.

Day 4

Spend the morning on the water. Book yourself on a **whale-watching tour** (p83) to Stellwagen Bank. Alternatively, get a closer view of the marine life inside the **New England Aquarium** (pictured; p83). Afterward, stroll along the **Rose Kennedy Greenway** (p81) stopping to admire the public art.

Continue along the Harborwalk, admiring the harbor views along the way. Your destination is the **Institute of Contemporary Art** (p76) for an afternoon of provocative contemporary art.

Continue your night on the town in the South End. Listen to some down and dirty blues at **Wally's Café** (p101) or sip cocktails with the sophisticates at **Beehive** (p101).

Need to Know

For detailed information, see Survival Guide p147

Currency
US dollar ($)

Language Spoken
English

Visas
Citizens of most countries are eligible for the Visa Waiver Program, which requires prior approval via Electronic System for Travel Authorization (ESTA).

Money
ATMs widely available. Credit cards accepted at most hotels, restaurants and shops.

Cell Phones
Most US cell-phone systems work on the GSM 850/1900 standard.

Time
Eastern Standard Time (GMT/UTC minus five hours)

Tipping
Tip at least 15% (more for good service) in all bars and restaurants.

Daily Budget

Budget: Less than $100
Dorm bed: $50
Pizza or dumplings: $5–10
Certain museum nights and walking tours: free
Ride on the T: $2.25–2.75

Midrange: $100–300
Double room in a midrange hotel: $150–250
Meal at a midrange restaurant: $15–25
Museum admission: $15–25
Short taxi ride: $15–20

Top End: More than $300
Double room in a top-end hotel: from $250
Meal at a top-end restaurant: from $25
Concerts, events and other activities: from $50

Useful Websites

Lonely Planet (www.lonelyplanet.com/usa/boston) Destination information, hotel bookings, traveler forum and more.

My Secret Boston (www.mysecretboston.com) Not *that* secret restaurants, nightlife, cultural and family events.

Blue Mass Group (www.bluemassgroup.com) Left-leaning political junkies report on State House goings-on.

Universal Hub (www.universalhub.com) Round-up of local news, with rich local commentary.

Arriving in Boston

Most visitors will arrive at Logan International Airport, or by train or bus at South Station (pictured). Both are easily accessible by subway, better known as the 'T', operated by the Massachusetts Bay Transportation Authority (MBTA).

✈ From Logan Airport

Around 3 miles east of central Boston, across the harbor in East Boston.

Bus Silver-line bus to South Station, 5:30am to 12:30am, free

Subway (The T) Blue-line subway to central Boston, $2.25 to $2.75

Taxi $25 or $30 to central Boston

🚌 From South Station

Located in central Boston.

Subway (The T) Red-line subway to almost anywhere in Boston, $2.25 to $2.75

Getting Around

S Subway (The T)

The MBTA (www.mbta.com) operates the USA's oldest subway, built in 1897 and known locally as the 'T'. There are four lines – red, blue, green and orange – that radiate from the principal downtown stations.

🚌 Bus

The MBTA (www.mbta.com) operates bus routes within the city. The silver line is a 'rapid' bus that is useful for Logan Airport (SL1) and the South End (SL4 or SL5).

🚲 Bicycle (Blue Bikes)

Boston's bike-share program is Blue Bikes (www.bluebikes.com). There are 200 Blue Bikes stations around Boston, Cambridge, Brookline and Somerville, stocked with 1800 bikes that are available for short-term loan.

Boston Neighborhoods

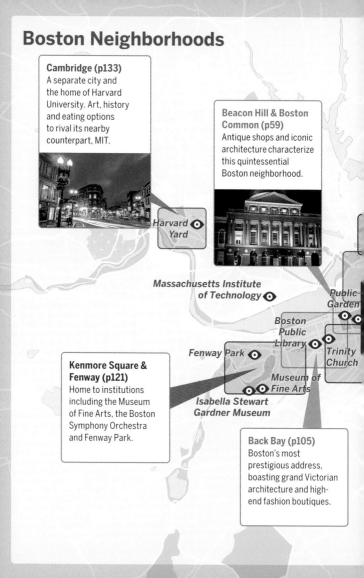

Cambridge (p133)
A separate city and the home of Harvard University. Art, history and eating options to rival its nearby counterpart, MIT.

Beacon Hill & Boston Common (p59)
Antique shops and iconic architecture characterize this quintessential Boston neighborhood.

Harvard Yard

Massachusetts Institute of Technology

Public Garden

Boston Public Library

Trinity Church

Fenway Park

Museum of Fine Arts

Isabella Stewart Gardner Museum

Kenmore Square & Fenway (p121)
Home to institutions including the Museum of Fine Arts, the Boston Symphony Orchestra and Fenway Park.

Back Bay (p105)
Boston's most prestigious address, boasting grand Victorian architecture and high-end fashion boutiques.

Charlestown (p33)
A historic neighborhood filled with architecture and war memorials.

West End & North End (p45)
Among the oldest parts of the city, this area is now home to a lively Italian immigrant population.

Boston Common

Institute of
⊙ Contemporary Art

Downtown & Seaport District (p75)
The hub of tourist activity, with historic sites, waterside walks and sightseeing boats.

South End & Chinatown (p93)
Overlapping districts offering authentic Asian food, sparkling theater marquees, cutting-edge art galleries and top-notch dining.

Explore
Boston

Worth a Trip 🔭

Boston's Walking Tours 🚶

Copley Square (p112) MARCIO SILVA/500PX/GETTY IMAGES ©

Explore ⊚
Charlestown

The site of the original settlement of the Massachusetts Bay Colony, Charlestown is the terminus for the Freedom Trail. Many tourists tromp across these historic cobblestone sidewalks to admire the USS Constitution and climb to the top of the Bunker Hill Monument, which towers above the neighborhood.

Short List

○ **Bunker Hill Monument (p35)** *Counting the 294 steps as you climb to the top and then catching your breath while you admire the 360-degree view.*

○ **Warren Tavern (p38)** *Sipping an ale at the same bar that propped up the founding fathers.*

○ **USS Constitution (p36)** *Hearing about the ship's long and storied history from US Navy sailors.*

○ **Pier Six (p39)** *Quaffing a beer or a cocktail while watching the sun set behind the city skyline.*

○ **USS Constitution Museum (p36)** *Experiencing the life of a sailor and admiring the model ship collection.*

Getting There & Around

Ⓜ The closest T stations are Community College (orange line) and North Station (junction of orange and green lines), both a 20-minute walk from the Charlestown sights.

⚓ The MBTA runs the Inner Harbor Ferry every 15 to 30 minutes between the Charlestown Navy Yard and Long Wharf on the Boston waterfront.

Neighborhood Map on p34

USS *Constitution* (p36) ROMAN BABAKIN/SHUTTERSTOCK ©

Sights

Bunker Hill Monument

MONUMENT

1  MAP P34, B1

This 220ft granite obelisk monument commemorates the turning-point battle that was fought on the surrounding hillside on June 17, 1775. Ultimately, the Redcoats prevailed, but the victory was bittersweet, as they lost more than one-third of their deployed forces, while the colonists suffered relatively few casualties. Climb the 294 steps to the top of the monument to enjoy the panorama of the city, the harbor and the North Shore. (☏617-242-7275; www.nps.gov/bost; Monument Sq; admission free; ⊗9am-5pm, to 6pm Jun-Sep; 🚌93 from Haymarket, Ⓣ Community College)

Bunker Hill Museum

MUSEUM

2  MAP P34, B2

Opposite the Bunker Hill Monument, this redbrick museum contains two floors of exhibits, including historical dioramas, a few artifacts and an impressive 360-degree mural depicting the battle. If you can find where the artist signed his masterpiece, you win a prize. (☏617-242-7275; www.nps.gov/bost; 43 Monument Sq; admission free; ⊗9am-5pm, to 6pm Jun-Sep; 🚌93 from Haymarket, Ⓣ Community College)

Statue of Colonel William Prescott and the Bunker Hill Monument

USS Constitution

SHIP

3 ⊙ MAP P34, D3

'Her sides are made of iron!' cried a crewman upon watching a shot bounce off the thick oak hull of the USS *Constitution* during the War of 1812. This bit of irony earned the legendary ship her nickname. Indeed, she has never gone down in a battle. The USS *Constitution* remains the oldest commissioned US Navy ship, dating to 1797, and she is normally taken out onto Boston Harbor every July 4 in order to maintain her commissioned status.

Make sure you bring a photo ID to go aboard. You'll learn lots, like how the captain's son died on her maiden voyage (an inauspicious start). (☏617-242-2543; www.navy.mil/local/constitution; Charlestown Navy Yard; admission free; ⊙10am-4pm Wed-Sun Jan-Mar, to 6pm Apr, 10am-6pm Tue-Sun May-Sep, to 5pm Oct-Dec; ♿; 🚌93 from Haymarket, ⛴Inner Harbor Ferry from Long Wharf, 🇹North Station)

USS Constitution Museum

MUSEUM

4 ⊙ MAP P34, D2

Head indoors to this museum for a play-by-play of the USS *Constitution*'s various battles, as well as her current role as the flagship of the US Navy. The exhibits on the War of 1812 and the Barbary War are especially interesting, and trace the birth of the US Navy during these relatively unknown conflicts. Upstairs, kids can experience what it was like to be a sailor on the USS *Constitution* in 1812. (☏617-426-1812; www.ussconstitutionmuseum.org; First Ave, Charlestown Navy Yard; suggested donation adult $10-15, child $5-10; ⊙9am-6pm Apr-Oct, 10am-5pm Nov-Mar; ♿; 🚌93 from Haymarket, ⛴Inner Harbor Ferry from Long Wharf, 🇹North Station)

Charlestown Navy Yard

HISTORIC SITE

5 ⊙ MAP P34, C3

Besides the historic ships docked here and the museum dedicated to them, the Charlestown Navy Yard is a living monument to its own history of shipbuilding and naval command. Visit the National Park Service Visitor Center located here for a free film, guided tours and other info about the Navy Yard and Freedom Trail sites. (☏617-242-5601; www.nps.gov/bost; admission free; ⊙visitor center 10am-5pm Wed-Sun Jan-Apr, 9am-5pm May-Sep, 10am-5pm Oct-Dec; 🚌93 from Haymarket, ⛴Inner Harbor Ferry from Long Wharf, 🇹North Station)

USS Cassin Young

SHIP

6 ⊙ MAP P34, D3

This 376ft WWII destroyer is one of 14 Fletcher-class destroyers built at the Charlestown Navy Yard. These were the Navy's fastest, most versatile ships. *Cassin Young* participated in the 1944 Battle of Leyte Gulf, as well as the 1945 invasion of Okinawa, during which the ship sustained two kamikaze hits, leaving 23 crew members dead and many more wounded. []Take a free 45-minute tour, or wander around the main deck on your own. (📞617-242-5601; Charlestown Navy Yard; admission free; 🕐10am-4:30pm May-Dec, to 5:30pm Jun-Sep; 🚌93 from Haymarket, ⛴Inner Harbor Ferry from Long Wharf, 🚇North Station)

Eating

Brewer's Fork
PIZZA $$

7 ❌ MAP P34, D1

This casual hipster hangout is a local favorite thanks to its enticing menu of small plates and pizzas, not to mention the excellent, oft-changing selection of about 30 craft beers. The wood-fired oven is the star of the show, but this place also does amazing things with its cheese and charcuterie boards. (📞617-337-5703; www.brewersfork. com; 7 Moulton St; small plates $8-14, pizzas $14-18; 🕐11:30am-10:30pm, to 11pm Thu-Sat, from 10:30am Sat & Sun; 🚌93 from Haymarket, ⛴Inner Harbor Ferry from Long Wharf, 🚇North Station)

Monument
GASTROPUB $$

8 ❌ MAP P34, A1

At long last, Charlestown is seeing some intriguing restaurants that cater to its foodie residents and visitors. The latest and greatest is Monument, with a gorgeous polished wood bar setting the scene. The menu is broad but tasty, ranging from cheeseburger sliders to

Climbing the Monument 📷

From April to June – due to the seasonal influx of school groups – you'll need a climbing pass before ascending the Bunker Hill Monument. Passes are available on a first-come, first-served at the Bunker Hill Museum across the street.

steamed Thai mussels and seared hanger steak. Brunch is particularly popular. (Lemon poppy-seed pancakes? Yes, please!) (📞617-337-5191; www.monumentcharlestown. com; 251 Main St; lunch $13-17, dinner $15-25; 🕐11:30am-midnight Mon-Fri, from 9am Sat & Sun; 🚇Community College)

Navy Yard Bistro & Wine Bar
FRENCH $$

9 ❌ MAP P34, D2

Dark and romantic, this hideaway is tucked into an off-street pedestrian walkway, allowing for comfortable outdoor seating in summer months. Inside, the cozy, carved-wood interior is an ideal date destination – perfect for hanger steak, braised short ribs and other old-fashioned favorites. The menu also features seasonal vegetables and excellent wines. (📞617-242-0036; www.navyyard bistro.com; cnr Second Ave & Sixth St; mains $18-36; 🕐4:30-9pm Sun-Tue, to 9:30pm Wed, to 10pm Thu-Sat; 🚌93 from Haymarket, ⛴Inner Harbor Ferry from Long Wharf, 🚇North Station)

Battle of Bunker Hill

(i)

'Don't fire until you see the whites of their eyes!' came the order from Colonel Prescott to revolutionary troops on June 17, 1775. Considering the ill-preparedness of the revolutionary soldiers, the bloody battle that followed resulted in a surprising number of British casualties. The Redcoats won the clash, but the colonists sustained comparatively few losses. Equally importantly, the battle demonstrated the gumption of the upstart revolutionaries.

The revolutionaries' biggest loss was General Joseph Warren, who was fighting on the front line and was killed by a musket shot to the head in the final British charge. A few weeks later, George Washington assumed command of the ragged Continental Army on the Cambridge Common.

Legal Oysteria

SEAFOOD $$

10 ✗ MAP P34, B3

Not an *osteria,* but an 'Oysteria.' Get it? This is seafood with an Italian twist, so you'll find dishes like Ligurian fish stew, swordfish *salmoriglio* and even roasted clam pizza. This place has a cool, modern atmosphere for a restaurant that's part of the Legal Sea Foods chain and is a welcome addition to the limited dining options in Charlestown. (✆617-712-1988; www.legalseafoods.com; 10 City Sq; mains $17-25; ⏱11:30am-11pm, to 1am Thu-Sat, from 10am Sun; ⌷93 from Haymarket, Ⓣ North Station)

Figs

PIZZA $$

11 ✗ MAP P34, B2

This creative pizzeria – which also has an outlet in Beacon Hill – is the brainchild of celebrity chef Todd English, who tops whisper-thin crusts with interesting, exotic toppings. Case in point: the namesake fig and prosciutto with Gorgonzola. The menu also includes sandwiches and fresh pasta. (✆617-242-2229; www.toddenglishsfigs.com; 67 Main St; mains $16-24; ⏱noon-2:30pm & 5-9:30pm Mon-Fri, noon-10pm Sat, noon-9:30pm Sun; ✗; Ⓣ Community College)

Drinking

Warren Tavern

PUB

12 🍺 MAP P34, B2

One of the oldest pubs in Boston, the Warren Tavern has been pouring pints for its customers since George Washington and Paul Revere drank here. It is named for General Joseph Warren, a fallen hero of the Battle of Bunker Hill (shortly after which – in 1780 – this pub was opened). Also recommended as a lunch stop (mains $14 to $20). (✆617-241-8142; www.warrentavern.com; 2 Pleasant St;

⏱11am-1am Mon-Fri, from 10am Sat & Sun; T Community College)

Pier Six
BAR

13 🚇 MAP P34, F3

At the end of the pier behind the Navy Yard, this understated tavern offers one of the loveliest views of the Boston Harbor and city skyline. The food is not that memorable, but it's a fine place to catch some rays on your face and the breeze off the water, and to enjoy an ice-cold one from behind the bar. (📞617-337-0054; www.pier6boston.com; 1 Eighth St, Pier 6; ⏱11am-1am; 🚌93 from Haymarket, ⛴Inner Harbor Ferry from Long Wharf, T North Station)

Zume's Coffee House
CAFE

14 🚇 MAP P34, A1

This is slightly off the beaten path (aka the Freedom Trail), but locals love it for the comfy leather chairs, specialty lattes and housemade English muffins. Also on the menu: soup, sandwiches and lunchy items. Paintings and photographs by local artists adorn the walls; children's books and tot-sized stools keep the kiddies happy. (www.zumescoffeehouse.com; 221 Main St; ⏱6am-4pm Mon-Fri, from 7am Sat & Sun; 📶♿; T Community College)

Warren Tavern

Walking Tour 🥾

Freedom Trail

Summon your inner Paul Revere and follow the red-brick road of the Freedom Trail, from the Boston Common to the Bunker Hill Monument. This 2.5-mile walking trail is the best introduction to revolutionary Boston, tracing the locations of the events that earned this town its status as the 'Cradle of Liberty.'

Walk Facts

Start Boston Common; T Park St

Finish Bunker Hill Monument; T Community College

Length 2.4 miles; three hours

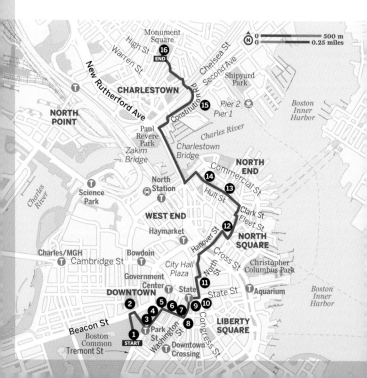

❶ Boston Common

The **Freedom Trail** (☏ 617-357-8300; www.thefreedomtrail.org) kicks off at the **Boston Common** (p60), America's oldest public park and a centerpiece of the city. The 50-acre green is crisscrossed with walking paths and dotted with monuments. Don't miss the powerful memorial to the victims of the Boston Massacre, erected in 1888.

❷ Massachusetts State House

Overlooking the Boston Common from the northeast corner, the **Massachusetts State House** (p68) occupies a proud spot atop the city's last remaining hill – land that was previously part of John Hancock's cow pasture. Other members of the Sons of Liberty (a clandestine network of patriots during the American Revolution) also had a hand in building the new capitol, literally: Samuel Adams and Paul Revere laid the cornerstones on July 4, 1795.

❸ Park Street Church

Just south of the State House, the soaring spire of **Park St Church** (☏ 617-523-3383; www.parkstreet.org; 1 Park St; ⏱ 9:30am-3pm Tue-Sat mid-Jun–Aug, Sun year-round; Ⓣ Park St) has been an unmistakable landmark since 1809. The church earned the moniker 'Brimstone Corner' both for its usage as a gunpowder storage place during the War of 1812 and for its fiery preaching.

❹ Granary Burying Ground

Walk north on Tremont St, where you will pass the Egyptian Revival gates of the **Granary Burying Ground** (p68). Steeped in history, the serene cemetery is the final resting place of many of the Sons of Liberty, as well as the victims of the Boston Massacre and other historical figures.

❺ King's Chapel & Burying Ground

Continue north to School St, where the Georgian **King's Chapel** (p81) overlooks its adjacent burying ground. It is perhaps an odd choice for inclusion on the Freedom Trail, since it was founded as an Anglican church in 1688. It does, however, contain a large bell crafted by Paul Revere, and the prestigious Governor's pew, once occupied by George Washington.

❻ Site of the First Public School

Turn east on School St, and take note of the bronze statue of Benjamin Franklin outside **Old City Hall** (☏ 617-204-9506; www.oldcityhall.com; 45 School St; Ⓣ State). A plaque commemorates this spot as the site of the country's first public school. Enter the courtyard to discover some of the school's distinguished alumni and some quirky artwork.

❼ Old Corner Bookstore

Continue east to the intersection of School St and Washington St. The little brick building on your left is known as the **Old Corner Bookstore** (Ⓣ Downtown Crossing), a literary and intellectual hot spot for 75 years. Strangely, it is now a Mexican fast-food joint.

❽ Old South Meeting House

Diagonally opposite across Washington St, the **Old South Meeting House** (p80) saw the beginnings of one of the American Revolution's most vociferous protests, the Boston Tea Party. Come off the street and listen to a reenactment of what went down that day.

❾ Old State House

Before the revolution, the seat of the Massachusetts government was the **Old State House** (p80), a redbrick colonial edifice that is now surrounded by modern buildings and busy streets. Inside, you can peruse historic artifacts and listen to firsthand accounts of revolutionary events. Outside, gaze up at the balcony, where the Declaration of Independence was first read to Bostonians in 1776.

❿ Boston Massacre Site

In front of the Old State House, the cobblestone circle marks the **site of the Boston Massacre** (p80), the revolution's first violent conflict, in 1770. On March 5, an angry crowd of protesters was throwing snowballs and rocks at the British soldiers, who eventually fired into the crowd, killing five.

⓫ Faneuil Hall

Nearly every visitor to Boston stops at Quincy Market to grab a beer or shop for souvenirs, but most bypass historic **Faneuil Hall** (p82), the original market and public meeting place that was built in 1740. Pause to admire the bronze statue of Samuel Adams, who sits astride his horse in Dock Sq. Then ascend to the 2nd-floor hall, where Adams was one of the many orators to speak out against British rule.

⓬ Paul Revere House

From Faneuil Hall, cross the Rose Kennedy Greenway and head up Hanover St into the heart of the North End. A zigzag right on to Richmond St and left on North St brings you to charming North Sq, once home to Paul Revere. The weathered clapboard house here – **Paul Revere House** (p50) – is the oldest example in Boston, as most other wooden buildings were destroyed by the fires that ravaged the city. This is likely where Paul Revere commenced his famous midnight ride.

⓭ Old North Church

Back on Hanover St, walk two blocks north to Paul Revere Mall. Besides a dramatic statue of the patriot himself, this park also provides a lovely vantage point to view your next destination, the **Old North Church** (p50). Boston's oldest house of worship, the 1723 church played a crucial role in revolutionary events. Take a breather in the delightful gardens behind the church.

⑭ Copp's Hill Burying Ground

From the church, head west on Hull St to **Copp's Hill Burying Ground** (p50). This quiet corner contains some of the city's oldest gravestones and offers grand views across the river to Charlestown. Find the headstone of Daniel Malcolm, which is littered with bullet holes from British troops who apparently took offense at his epitaph. Incidentally, little is known about Malcolm's actual role in protests or revolution; historical records only show that he was arrested for failing to pay duty on 60 casks of wine.

⑮ USS *Constitution*

Continue west on Hull St to its end. Turn left on Commercial St and walk across the Charlestown Bridge. Turning right on Constitution Rd brings you to the Charlestown Navy Yard, home of the world's oldest commissioned warship, the **USS Constitution** (p36). Board the ship for a tour of the upper decks, where you will learn about its exploits in America's earliest naval battles.

⑯ Bunker Hill Monument

Walk through the winding cobblestone streets up to the 220ft granite obelisk that is the **Bunker Hill Monument** (p35). Check out the dioramas in the museum to better understand what transpired on that fateful day in June 1775, when the Battle of Bunker Hill took place. Then climb 294 steps to the top of the monument to enjoy the panorama of the city, the harbor and the North Shore.

Explore ⊙

West End & North End

Although the West End and North End are physically adjacent, they are atmospherically worlds apart. The West End is an institutional area without much zest. By contrast, the North End is delightfully spicy, thanks to the many Italian ristoranti and salumerie (delis) that line the streets.

Short List

○ **Pomodoro (p52)** *Squeezing into a candlelit table in the North End for amazing Italian food and service.*

○ **Alibi (p54)** *Sipping a cocktail and appreciating the irony that this former jailhouse is now a luxury hotel.*

○ **Old North Church (p50)** *Gazing at the steeple and imagining the lanterns signaling the approach of the British Regulars (soldiers).*

○ **Museum of Science (p50)** *Discovering science at work in your own body in the interactive Hall of Human Life.*

○ **Paul Revere House (p50)** *Exploring the quaint, cramped quarters at Boston's oldest house, once home to one of the celebrated Sons of Liberty.*

Getting There & Around

Ⓜ For the West End, use the red line Charles/MGH to access sites along Cambridge St. At the junction of the green and orange lines, North Station is more convenient for the northern part of the neighborhood. For the North End, the closest T station is Haymarket, which lies on both the green and orange lines.

Neighborhood Map on p48

North End and the steeple of the Old North Church (p50)
SEAN PAVONE/SHUTTERSTOCK ©

Walking Tour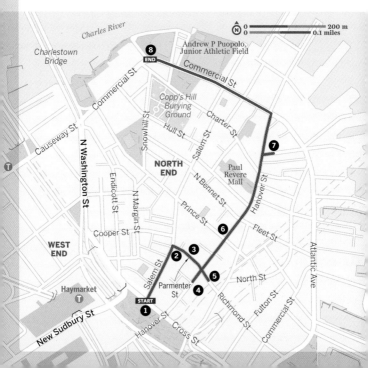

Italian Culture in the North End

The North End's warren of alleyways retains the Old World flavor brought by Italian immigrants, ever since they started settling here in the early 20th century. And when we say 'flavor,' we're not being metaphorical. We mean garlic, basil and oregano, sautéed in extra-virgin olive oil; rich tomato sauces that have simmered for hours; amaretto and anise; and delicious creamy gelato.

Walk Facts

Start Haymarket;
[T] Haymarket

Finish Langone Park;
[T] North Station

Length 1 mile; 30 to 60 minutes

❶ North End Park

Grab a snack from **Maria's Pastry** (www.mariaspastry.com; 46 Cross St; pastries $3-5; ⏱7am-7pm Mon-Sat, to 5pm Sun; 🖪), then cross the street to sit in the shade under grape vines in **North End Park** (www.rosekennedy greenway.org), designed as the neighborhood's 'front porch.'

❷ Polcari's Coffee

Duck into **Polcari's Coffee** (www. polcariscoffee.com; 105 Salem St; ⏱10am-6pm Mon-Fri, from 9am Sat) and take in the delightful aroma of imported coffee beans, tea leaves and aromatic spices. Founded in 1932, this old-fashioned dry-goods store hearkens back to the early 20th century, when Italian immigration was at its peak.

❸ North End Branch Library

Most Italian immigrants to Boston came from southern Italy and especially Sicily. But the **local library** (☎617-227-8135; www.bpl.org/branches/north.php; 25 Parmenter St; ⏱10am-6pm Mon, Tue & Thu, noon-8pm Wed, 9am-5pm Fri, 9am-2pm Sat; T Haymarket) in the North End contains an unexpected souvenir of northern Italy – a model of the Palazzo Ducale in Venice.

❹ Caffè Paradiso

Stop in at this classic **cafe** (www. caffeparadisoboston.com; 255 Hanover St; ⏱7am-2am; 🛜; T Haymarket) for cappuccino and neighborhood vibes. Regulars watch Italian football on TV while the bartender masterfully pours neat cognacs with understated finesse.

❺ Salumeria Italiana

Salumeria Italiana (www. salumeriaitaliana.com; 151 Richmond St; ⏱8am-7pm Mon-Sat, 10am-4pm Sun; T Haymarket) has been doing its thing for more than 50 years – supplying locals with imported products like high-quality balsamic vinegar and extra virgin olive oil.

❻ St Leonard's Church

Dating to 1873, **St Leonard's Church** (☎617-523-2110; www. saintleonardchurchboston.org; 320 Hanover St; ⏱9:30am-2:30pm; T Haymarket) was founded and built by Italian immigrants. It still holds weekly Mass in Italian, as well as in English.

❼ All Saints Way

Local collector and devout Catholic Peter Baldassari has been collecting holy cards for nearly 80 years. His treasures are on display in this tiny alleyway off Battery St, locally known as **All Saints Way** (4 Battery St; T Haymarket).

❽ Langone Park

It was a sad day in North End history when, in 1919, a distillery tank burst and the neighborhood was flooded with molasses (p56). The site of this disaster is now **Langone Park** (☎617-626-1250; Commercial St), a peaceful place for neighbors to congregate and play bocce.

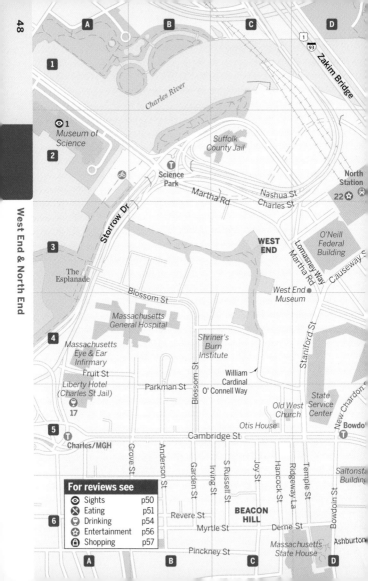

1 Zakim Bridge

Charles River

⊙1 Museum of Science

2

Suffolk County Jail

🚲 Science Park

T

North Station

22☆

Martha Rd

Nashua St
Charles St

WEST END

O'Neill Federal Building

3

Storrow Dr

The Esplanade

Blossom St

West End Museum

Lomasney Way

Martha Rd

Causeway St

Staniford St

Massachusetts General Hospital

Shriner's Burn Institute

4

Massachusetts Eye & Ear Infirmary

Fruit St

Liberty Hotel (Charles St Jail)

🏠17

Parkman St

Blossom St

William Cardinal O'Connell Way

Old West Church

State Service Center

New Chardon St

Bowdoin

T

Otis House

5 **T** Charles/MGH

Cambridge St

Grove St

Anderson St

Garden St

Irving St

S Russell St

Joy St

Hancock St

Ridgeway La

Temple St

Bowdoin St

Saltonstall Building

BEACON HILL

Revere St

Myrtle St

Derne St

Ashburton

For reviews see

⊙	Sights	p50
✕	Eating	p51
🍷	Drinking	p54
☆	Entertainment	p56
🔒	Shopping	p57

6

Pinckney St

Massachusetts State House

A B C D

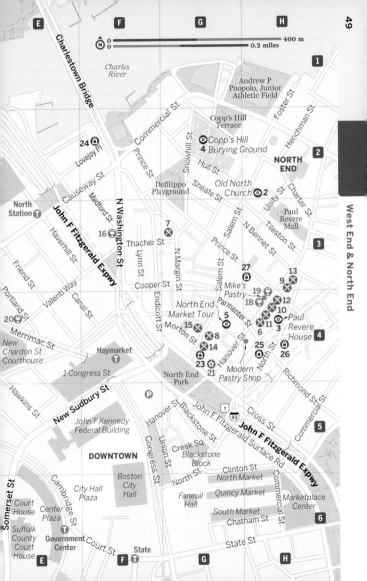

West End & North End

400 m
0.2 miles

Charles River

Charlestown Bridge

Andrew P Puopolo, Junior Athletic Field

Copp's Hill Terrace

Copp's Hill Burying Ground 4

NORTH END

Commercial St

24

Lovejoy Pl

Causeway St

Medford St

N Washington St

Prince St

Snowhill St

Hull St

Sheafe St

Defilippo Playground

Old North Church 2

North Station

John F Fitzgerald Expwy

Haverhill St

Friend St

Portland St

Valenti Way

Canal St

Thacher St

Lynn St

Cooper St

N Margin St

7

16

Salem St

N Bennet St

Prince St

Tileston St

Unity St

Charter St

Paul Revere Mall

27

Mike's Pastry

19

18

Parmenter St

13

9

12

10

11

6

Paul Revere House 3

5

North End Market Tour

15

8

14

23

21

Morton St

Hanover St

25

26

Endicott St

Merrimac St

20

New Chardon St Courthouse

Haymarket

1 Congress St

North End Park

Modern Pastry Shop

Richmond St

Hawkins St

New Sudbury St

John F Kennedy Federal Building

P

Hanover St

Blackstone St

Cross St

John F Fitzgerald Surface Rd

John F Fitzgerald Expwy

93

Commercial St

DOWNTOWN

Congress St

Union St

Creek Sq

Blackstone Block

Clinton St

North Market

Marketplace Center

Somerset St

Court House

Center Plaza

City Hall Plaza

Boston City Hall

North St

Faneuil Hall

Quincy Market

Suffolk County Court House

Government Center

Cambridge St

Court St

State

South Market

Chatham St

State St

Commercial St

Cambridge St

Sights

Museum of Science · MUSEUM

1 ◎ MAP P48, A2

This educational playground has more than 600 interactive exhibits. Favorites include the world's largest lightning-bolt generator, a full-scale space capsule, a world population meter and an impressive dinosaur exhibit. Kids go wild exploring computers and technology, maps and models, birds and bees, and human evolution. Don't miss the **Hall of Human Life**, where the visitors can witness the hatching of baby chicks. The **Discovery Center** is a hands-on play area for kids under the age of eight. (☎617-723-2500; www.mos.org; Charles River Dam; museum admission adult/child $28/23, planetarium adult/child $10/8, theater adult/child $10/8; ☺9am-7pm Sat-Thu Jul & Aug, to 5pm Sep-Jun, to 9pm Fri year-round; P🚻; Ⓣ Science Park/West End)

Old North Church · CHURCH

2 ◎ MAP P48, H2

Longfellow's poem 'Paul Revere's Ride' has immortalized this graceful church. It was here, on the night of April 18, 1775, that the sexton hung two lanterns from the steeple as a signal that the British would advance on Lexington and Concord via the sea route. Also called Christ Church, this 1723 Anglican place of worship is Boston's oldest church. (Christ Church; ☎617-858-8231; www.oldnorth.com; 193 Salem St; adult/child $8/4, plus $2 for tour; ☺10am-4pm Nov-March, 9am-6pm April-Oct; Ⓣ Haymarket, North Station)

Paul Revere House · HISTORIC SITE

3 ◎ MAP P48, H4

When silversmith Paul Revere rode to warn patriots of the British march to Lexington and Concord, he set out from this home on North Sq. This small clapboard house was built in 1680, making it the oldest house in Boston. A self-guided tour through the house and courtyard gives a glimpse of what life was like for the Revere family (which included 16 children!). (☎617-523-2338; www.paulreverehouse.org; 19 North Sq; adult/child $4.50/1; ☺9:30am-5:15pm mid-Apr–Oct, to 4:15pm Nov–mid-Apr, closed Mon Jan-Mar; Ⓣ Haymarket)

Copp's Hill Burying Ground · CEMETERY

4 ◎ MAP P48, G2

The city's second-oldest cemetery – dating to 1660 – is the final resting place for an estimated 10,000 souls. It is named for William Copp, who originally owned this land. While the oldest graves belong to Copp's children, there are several other noteworthy residents. (Hull St; ☺8am-5pm; Ⓣ North Station)

North End Market Tour · WALKING

5 ◎ MAP P48, G4

A three-hour tour around the North End that includes shopping in a salumeria, sampling pastries at the local pasticceria, smelling the herbs and spices that flavor Italian cooking, and sampling spirits at an enoteca (wine bar). Guests have the opportunity to chat with local shopkeepers and other longtime North End residents about living and eating in this food-rich neighborhood. (☏617-523-6032; www.bostonfoodtours.com; tours $60; ⏱tours 10am & 2pm Wed & Sat, 10am & 3pm Fri)

Eating

Galleria Umberto PIZZA $

6 ✕ MAP P48, H4

Paper plates, cans of soda, Sicilian pizza. This lunchtime legend (and 2018 James Beard Award winner!) closes as soon as the slices are gone. And considering their thick and chewy goodness, that's often before the official 3pm closing time. Loyal patrons line up early so they're sure to get theirs. Cash only. (☏617-227-5709; www.galleria umbertonorthend.com; 289 Hanover St; mains $2-5; ⏱11am-3pm Mon-Sat; ⚄; Ⓣ Haymarket)

Pizzeria Regina PIZZA $

7 ✕ MAP P48, G3

The queen of North End pizzerias is the legendary Pizzeria Regina, famous for brusque but endearing waitstaff and crispy, thin-crust pizza. Thanks to the slightly spicy sauce (flavored with aged Romano cheese), Regina repeatedly wins accolades for its pies, including recognition by a certain unmentionable travel website

Museum of Science

West End & North End Eating

West End Museum

The West End – formerly a vibrant ethnic neighborhood – was razed by 'urban renewal' in the 1950s. Now it's dominated by concrete monoliths and institutional buildings. The **West End Museum** (Map p48, D3; ☏617-723-2125; www.thewestendmuseum.org; 150 Staniford St; admission free; ◷noon-5pm Tue-Fri, 11am-4pm Sat; Ⓣ North Station) is dedicated to preserving the memory of the neighborhood and educating the public about the ramifications of unchecked urban development. The main exhibit *The Last Tenement* traces the history of the neighborhood from 1850 to 1958, highlighting its immigrant populations, economic evolution and eventual destruction.

as the best pizza *in the country*. Worth the wait. (☏617-227-0765; www.pizzeriaregina.com; 11½ Thacher St; pizzas $13-24; ◷11am-11:30pm Sun-Thu, to 12:30am Fri & Sat; ✐; Ⓣ Haymarket)

Pauli's
SANDWICHES $

8 🍴 MAP P48, G4

If you're in the mood for a 'lobsta roll,' head to Pauli's for 7oz of pink succulent goodness, stuffed into a lightly grilled hot-dog roll – just the way it's meant to be. The menu of sandwiches is extensive and most of them are tasty; the California wrap is popular among the health-conscious. (☏857-284-7064; www.paulisnorthend.com; 65 Salem St; mains $7-20; ◷8am-9pm Mon-Fri, 10am-9pm Sat, to 5pm Sun; 🛜✐; Ⓣ Haymarket)

Pomodoro
ITALIAN $$

9 🍴 MAP P48, H3

Seductive Pomodoro offers a super-intimate, romantic setting

(reservations are essential). The food is simple but perfectly pre-pared: fresh pasta, spicy tomato sauce, grilled fish and meats, and wine by the glass. If you're lucky, you might be on the receiving end of a complimentary tiramisu for dessert. Cash only. (☏617-367-4348; 351 Hanover St; mains $22-26; ◷5:30-11pm; Ⓣ Haymarket)

Scopa
ITALIAN $$

10 🍴 MAP P48, H4

Every meal at Scopa starts with delectable, warm Italian flatbread, served with a selection of olive oils for dipping. This is just a teaser of the delights to come, which might include Venetian meatballs or porcini mushroom risotto. The atmosphere is intimate and service is consistently excellent. (☏857-317-2871; www.scopaboston.com; 319 Hanover St; mains $19-28; ◷11am-11pm; Ⓣ Haymarket)

53

West End & North End Eating

Carmelina's
ITALIAN $$

11 MAP P48, H4

There's a lot to look at when you sit down at Carmelina's, whether you face the busy open kitchen or the massive windows overlooking Hanover St. This understated, contemporary space serves up Sicilian dishes with a modern American twist – customers are crazy about the Crazy Alfredo and the Sunday Macaroni (which is served every day, in case you're wondering). (617-742-0020; www.carmelinasboston.com; 307 Hanover St; mains $18-29; noon-10pm; ; Haymarket)

Daily Catch
SEAFOOD $$

12 MAP P48, H4

Although owner Paul Freddura long ago added a few tables and an open kitchen, this shoebox fish joint still retains the atmosphere of a retail fish market (complete with chalkboard menu and wine served in plastic cups). Fortunately, it also retains the freshness of the fish. The specialty is *tinta de calamari* (squid-ink pasta). Cash only. (617-523-8567; http://thedailycatch.com; 323 Hanover St; mains $18-25; 11am-10pm; Haymarket)

Giacomo's Ristorante
ITALIAN $$

13 MAP P48, H3

Customers line up before the doors open so they can guarantee themselves a spot in the first round of seating at this North End favorite. Enthusiastic and entertaining waitstaff plus cramped quarters ensure that you get to know your neighbors. The cuisine is no-frills southern Italian fare, served in unbelievable portions. Cash only. (617-523-9026; 355 Hanover St; mains $15-20; 4:30-10pm Mon-Thu, to 10:30pm Fri & Sat, 4-9:30pm Sun; ; Haymarket)

Neptune Oyster
SEAFOOD $$$

14 MAP P48, G4

Neptune's menu hints at Italian, but you'll also find elements of Mexican, French, Southern and old-fashioned New England. The impressive raw bar and daily seafood specials confirm that this is not your traditional North End eatery. Reservations are not accepted so come early and be prepared to wait. The retro interior offers a convivial - if crowded - setting, with an excellent option for solo diners at the marble bar. (617-742-3474; www.neptuneoyster.com; 63 Salem St; mains $19-39; 11:30am-9:30pm Sun-Thu, to 10:30pm Fri & Sat; Haymarket)

TreMonte
ITALIAN $$$

15 MAP P48, G4

Customers are raving about this North End newcomer, which serves classic northern Italian fare in its sophisticated dining room with big windows overlooking Salem St. Indulge in favorites like chicken parmigiana and

Mikes vs Modern 🍴

Only slightly less tempestuous than the rivalry between the Red Sox and the Yankees is the rivalry between **Mike's Pastry** (Map p48, H4; 📞617-742-3050; www.mikespastry.com; 300 Hanover St; pastries $3-5; ⏰8am-10pm Sun-Thu, to 11pm Fri & Sat; 🚇Haymarket) and **Modern Pastry** (Map p48, H4; 📞617-523-3783; www.modernpastry.com; 257 Hanover St; sweets $2-4; ⏰8am-10pm Sun-Thu, to 11pm Fri, to midnight Sat; 🚇Haymarket), only a block apart on Hanover St. If you have time to wait in line, you might as well sample both and decide for yourself. If you don't have time to wait in line, go to **Maria's** (p47) instead.

grilled pork chops, with a nice selection of Italian wines (but no hard liquor). Impeccable service makes the place stand out. (📞617-530-1955; www.tremonterestaurant.com; 76 Salem St; mains $18-32; ⏰4-10pm Mon-Thu, to 11pm Fri, 11:30am-11pm Sat, to 10pm Sun; 🚇Haymarket)

Drinking

Ward 8 COCKTAIL BAR

16 🚇 MAP P48, F3

The bartenders at this throwback know their stuff, mixing up a slew of specialty cocktails (including the namesake Ward 8) and serving them in clever thematic containers. The menu also features craft beers and tempting New American cuisine (try the sesame chili duck wings). The atmosphere is classy but convivial, and unique in the West End. (📞617-823-4478; www.ward8.com; 90 N Washington St; ⏰11:30am-1am Mon-Wed, to 2am Thu & Fri, 10am-2am Sat, to 1am Sun; 🚇North Station, Haymarket)

Alibi COCKTAIL BAR

17 🚇 MAP P48, A5

Housed in the former Charles St Jail, this hot-to-trot drinking venue is in the old 'drunk tank' (holding cell for the intoxicated). The prison theme is played up, with mug shots hanging on the brick walls, and iron bars on the doors and windows. Prices are high and service can be lacking, but it's fun to drink in jail. Dress sharp. (📞857-241-1144; www.alibiboston.com; 215 Charles St, Liberty Hotel; ⏰5pm-2am; 🚇Charles/MGH)

Caffè Vittoria CAFE

18 🚇 MAP P48, H4

A delightful destination for dessert or aperitifs, this frilly parlor displays antique espresso machines and black-and-white photos, with a pressed-tin ceiling reminiscent of the Victorian era. Grab a marble-topped table, order a cappuccino and enjoy the romantic setting. Cash only, just like the olden days. (☎617-227-7606; www.caffevittoria.com; 290-296 Hanover St; ⏰7am-midnight Sun-Thu, to 12:30pm Fri & Sat; 📶; 🇹Haymarket)

Caffè Dello Sport

19 🚇 MAP P48, H4

An informal crowd of thick-accented guys from the 'hood sit at glass-topped tables and drink espresso and Campari. This is a great place to watch a football game (and yes, we mean soccer) – or just to watch the other patrons. They also make a mean *cannoli*. Cash only. (☎617-523-5063; www.caffedellosport.net; 308 Hanover St; ⏰6am-11:30pm Mon-Thu,

to 12:30pm Fri, 7am-12:30pm Sat & Sun; 📶; 🇹Haymarket)

West End Johnnies

20 🚇 MAP P48, E4

West End Johnnies is a grown-up sports bar, with black leather furniture and retro sports paraphernalia adorning the walls. On weekend nights, it's also a dance club. And most importantly, on Sundays, it's a great brunch destination.

No matter where you spent your Saturday night, JC's corned-beef hash and eggs and live reggae music make for an excellent way to recover. (☎617-227-1588; www.

Mike's Pastry

The Great Molasses Flood

For years Boston was a leader in the production and export of rum, made from West Indian sugar cane. Near the water's edge in the North End stood a storage tank for the Purity Distilling Company. On a January morning in 1919, the large tank, filled to the brim with brown molasses, suddenly began shuddering and rumbling as its bindings came undone.

The pressure caused the tank to explode, spewing 2 million gallons of molasses into the city like a volcano. The sweet explosion leveled surrounding tenements, knocked buildings off their foundations and wiped out a loaded freight train. Panic-stricken, people and animals fled the deadly ooze. A molasses wave surged down the streets drowning all in its sticky path. The Great Molasses Flood killed a dozen horses and 21 people, and injured more than 100. The clean up lasted nearly six months. *Dark Tide,* by journalist Stephen Puleo, provides a fascinating account of the causes and controversy surrounding this devastating explosion.

westendjohnnies.com; 138 Portland St; 4pm-2am Tue-Sat, 11am-4pm Sun; North Station)

Entertainment

Improv Asylum   COMEDY

21 MAP P48, G4

A basement theater is somehow the perfect setting for the dark humor spewing from the mouths of this offbeat crew. No topic is too touchy, no politics too correct. Shows vary from night to night, but the standard Mainstage Show mixes up the improv with comedy sketches that are guaranteed to make you giggle. The Saturday midnight show is aptly named 'Raunchy.' (617-263-6887; www.improvasylum.com; 216 Hanover St; tickets $10-28; shows 8pm Sun-Thu, 7:30pm, 10pm & midnight Fri & Sat; Haymarket)

TD Garden   STADIUM

22 MAP P48, D2

TD Garden is home to the NHL Boston Bruins, who play hockey here from September to June, and the NBA Boston Celtics, who play basketball from October to April. It's the city's largest venue, so big-name musicians perform here, too. (event info 617-624-1000; www.tdgarden.com; 150 Causeway St; North Station)

Shopping

Salmagundi
HATS

23 MAP P48, G4

While the flagship Salmagundi store in Jamaica Plain has a bigger selection, this second location in the North End still offers some 4000 hats for your head-topping pleasure. (617-936-4015; www.salmagundiboston.com; 61 Salem St; 11am-7pm Tue-Fri, to 8pm Sat, to 6pm Sun & Mon; T Haymarket)

Converse at Lovejoy Wharf
SHOES

24 MAP P48, F2

Occupying the ground level of the Converse world headquarters, this flagship store has a sweet selection of its classic sneakers, including some true originals. Look for a handful of styles with Boston themes – 'Exclusive at Lovejoy Wharf' as they say. (617-377-1000; www.converse.com; 140 N Washington St; 10am-7pm Mon-Sat, 11am-6pm Sun; T North Station)

North Bennet Street School
ARTS & CRAFTS

25 MAP P48, H4

The North Bennet Street School has been training craftspeople for over 100 years, offering programs in traditional skills like bookbinding, woodworking and locksmithing. The school's on-site gallery sells pieces made by students and alumni. (617-227-0155; www.nbss.edu; 150 North St; 9:30am-5:30pm Mon-Fri; T Haymarket)

I Am Books
BOOKS

26 MAP P48, H4

Calling itself 'an Italian-American cultural hub,' this small independent bookstore is the perfect place to pick up reading materials for an upcoming trip to Italy. Specializing in fiction set in Italy and nonfiction about Italy. (857-263-7665; www.iambooksboston.com; 189 North St; 10am-6pm Mon-Sat, to 5pm Sun; T Haymarket)

Sedurre
CLOTHING

27 MAP P48, H3

If you speak Italian, you'll know that Sedurre's thing is sexy and stylish. (It means 'seduce.') The shop started with fine lingerie. Sisters Robyn and Daria were so good at that, they created an additional space next door for dresses, evening wear and jewelry.(617-720-4400; www.sedurreboston.com; 28½ Prince St; 11am-7pm Mon-Wed, to 8pm Thu & Fri, to 9pm Sat, noon-6pm Sun; T Haymarket)

Explore ◎
Beacon Hill &
Boston Common

Abutted by the Boston Common – the nation's original public park and the centerpiece of the city – and topped with the gold-domed Massachusetts State House, Beacon Hill is the neighborhood most often featured on Boston postcards. The retail and residential streets on Beacon Hill are delightfully, quintessentially Boston.

Short List

◦ **Public Garden (p64)** *Breathing in the sweet smell of flowering trees and blooming beds of seasonal blooms.*

◦ **Boston Common (p60)** *Packing a picnic for an afternoon of frolicking or an evening of outdoor theater.*

◦ **Charles Street (p71)** *Browsing for trash and treasure in the antique shops and sweet boutiques.*

◦ **Black Heritage Trail (p68)** *Learning about the early African American settlement on Beacon Hill.*

◦ **Massachusetts State House (p68)** *Searching for the Sacred Cod, the Holy Mackerel and other iconic emblems.*

Getting There & Around

Ⓜ At the junction of the red and green lines, Park St T station services the Boston Common and sights in the southeastern part of Beacon Hill. Also on the red line, Charles/MGH T station is convenient to Charles St, Cambridge St and the Charles River Esplanade.

Neighborhood Map on p66

Massachusetts State House (p68) CO LEONG/SHUTTERSTOCK ©

Top Experience 📷
People Watch on Boston Common

The 50-acre Boston Common is the country's oldest public park. The Common has served many purposes over the years, including as a campground for British troops during the Revolutionary War and as green grass for cattle grazing until the 1830s. Although there is still a grazing ordinance on the books, the Common today serves picnickers, sunbathers and people-watchers.

◉ MAP P66, E4

btwn Tremont, Charles, Beacon & Park Sts

🕑 6am-midnight

🅿 🚻

Ⓣ Park St

Blaxton Plaque

In 1634 William Blaxton sold a piece of land for £30 so the Massachusetts Bay Colony would have a place for cows to graze. Such was the inglorious beginning of the Boston Common, the country's oldest public park. This **plaque** is emblazoned with the words of the treaty between Governor Winthrop and Mr Blaxton, should you care to know the details.

Brewer Fountain

This bronze beauty dates to 1868, when it was gifted to the city of Boston by the wealthy merchant Gardner Brewer. The lovely **fountain** features four aquatic deities from antiquity: the Roman god of water, Neptune; the Greek sea goddess, Amphitrite; and the spirit Acis and the sea nymph Galatea, both from *Metamorphoses*, by the Roman poet Ovid. The design won a gold medal at the 1855 World's Fair.

Robert Gould Shaw Memorial

It took Augustus Saint-Gaudens nearly 13 years to sculpt this magnificent **bas-relief memorial** (cnr Beacon & Park Sts) honoring the 54th Massachusetts Regiment of the Union Army, the nation's first all-black Civil War regiment (depicted in the 1989 film *Glory*). These soldiers steadfastly refused their monthly stipend for nearly two years, until Congress increased it to match the amount that white regiments received. Shaw and half his men were killed in a battle at Fort Wagner, South Carolina. The National Park Service (NPS) tour of the **Black Heritage Trail** (617-742-5415; www.nps.gov/boaf; tours 1pm Mon-Sat, more frequently in summer; Park St) departs from here.

Boston Massacre Monument

This 25ft **monument** pays tribute to the five victims of the Boston Massacre, which took

o The on-site **information kiosk** (GBCVB Visitors Center; Map p66, F4; 617-426-3115; www.bostonusa.com; 8:30am-5pm Mon-Fri, from 9am Sat & Sun; Park St) is a great source of information, maps etc.

o The kiosk is also the starting place for guided tours by the **Freedom Trail Foundation** (617-357-8300; www.thefreedomtrail.org; adult/child $14/8; Park St).

o The Boston Common is often called 'the Common' in local parlance, but never 'the Commons.' Use the singular or risk ridicule by locals!

✕ Take a Break

Various food trucks park near the entrance to the Park St T station. **Bon Me** (www.bonmetruck.com) is a favorite.

Alternatively, check out the Earl of Sandwich (p65), located in the handsome 'Pink Palace.'

place down the street in front of the Old State House. The monument replicates Paul Revere's famous engraving of the tragic event. Revere's effective propaganda depicts the soldiers shooting down defenseless colonists in cold blood, when in reality they were reacting to the aggressive crowd in self-defense.

Soldiers & Sailors Monument

Dedicated in 1877, this massive **monument** atop Flagstaff Hill pays tribute to the namesake soldiers and sailors who died in the Civil War. The four bronze statues represent Peace, the female figure looking to the South; the Sailor, the seaman looking toward the ocean; History, the Greek figure looking to heaven; and the Soldier, an infantryman standing at ease. See if you can recognize the many historical figures in the elaborate bronze reliefs.

Frog Pond

When temperatures drop, the Boston Common becomes an urban winter wonderland, with slipping and sliding, swirling and twirling on the **Frog Pond** (☎617-635-2120; www.bostonfrogpond.com; adult/child $6/free, skate rental $12/6; ☻10am-3:45pm Mon, to 9pm Tue-Thu & Sun, to 10pm Fri & Sat mid-Nov–mid-Mar; ⛄; ⓣPark St). Weekends are often crowded, as are weekdays around noon, as local skate fiends spend their lunch break on the ice. In warmer weather, the Frog Pond becomes a wet and wild spray pool where kids can cool off.

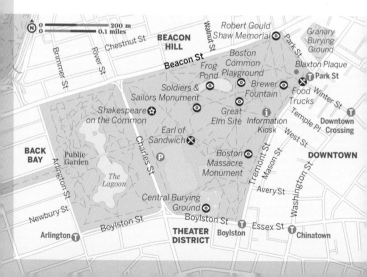

Boston Massacre

In front of the Old State House, encircled by cobblestones, a bronze plaque marks the spot where the first blood was shed for the American independence movement.

On March 5, 1770, an angry mob of colonists swarmed the British soldiers guarding the State House. Sam Adams, John Hancock and about 40 other protesters hurled snowballs, rocks and insults. Thus provoked, the soldiers fired into the crowd and killed five townspeople, including Crispus Attucks, a former slave.

The incident sparked enormous anti-British sentiment. Paul Revere helped fan the flames by widely disseminating an engraving that depicted the scene as an unmitigated slaughter. Interestingly, John Adams and Josiah Quincy – both of whom opposed the heavy-handed authoritarian British rule – defended the accused soldiers in court, and seven of the nine were acquitted.

Tadpole Playground

We're not sure if America's first public park is home to its first playground, but rest assured, the **Tadpole Playground** has a huge playscape which gets overrun with kids. There's also a carousel nearby.

Shakespeare on the Common

Each summer, the **Commonwealth Shakespeare Company** (✏617-426-0863; www.commshakes. org; Boston Common; ◷Jul & Aug; Ⓣ Park St) stages a major production on the Boston Common, drawing crowds for (free) Shakespeare under the stars. Productions often appeal to the masses with a populist twist, thus *The Taming of the Shrew,* set in a North End restaurant.

Central Burying Ground

Dating to 1756, the **Central Burying Ground** (Boylston St; ◷9am-5pm; Ⓣ Boylston) is the least celebrated of the old cemeteries, as it was the burial ground of the down-and-out (according to an account in Edwin Bacon's *Boston Illustrated,* it was used for 'Roman Catholics and strangers dying in the town'). Some reports indicate that it contains an unmarked mass grave for British soldiers who died in the Battle of Bunker Hill. The most recognized name here is the artist-in-residence Gilbert Stuart. Sometimes called the 'Father of American Portraiture,' Stuart painted the portrait of George Washington that now graces the dollar bill.

Top Experience 📷
Take a Breather in the Public Garden

The Public Garden is a 24-acre botanical oasis of Victorian flowerbeds, blooming rose gardens, verdant grass and weeping willow trees shading a tranquil lagoon. Until it was filled in the early 19th century, it was (like Back Bay) a tidal salt marsh. Now, at any time of the year, it is awash with seasonal blooms, gold-toned leaves or untrammeled snow.

◎ MAP P66, C4

📞 617-723-8144

www.friendsofthepublic
garden.org

Arlington St

🕐 dawn-dusk

🚻

🇹 Arlington

Monuments

At the main entrance (from Arlington St), visitors are greeted by a **statue of George Washington** looking stately atop his horse.

Other pieces of public art are more whimsical; the most endearing is **Make Way for Ducklings** (T Arlington), always a favorite with tiny tots who can climb and sit on the bronze ducks. The sculpture depicts Mrs Mallard and her eight ducklings, the main characters in the beloved book by Robert McCloskey.

The small-scale fountains also have fun, kid-friendly themes. See if your children can find **Boy and Bird** by Bashka Paeff or **Triton Babies** by Anna Coleman Ladd.

On the northwest side of the lagoon, the **Ether Monument** commemorates the first use of anesthesia for medical purposes, which took place in Boston. Dating to 1868, it is the oldest monument in the garden. The bronze figures tell the story of the Good Samaritan.

Nearby, **Angel of the Waters** (pictured left) is a bronze and granite beauty, created by Daniel Chester French in 1924 and restored in 2016. It is a tribute to the local philanthropist George Robert White.

Swan Boats

The story of the **swan boats** (📞617-522-1966; www.swanboats.com; adult/child $4/2.50; ⏲10am-4pm Apr-Jun, to 5pm Jul-Aug) goes back to 1877, when Robert Paget developed a catamaran with a pedal-powered paddlewheel. Inspired by the opera *Lohengrin,* in which a heroic knight rides across a river in a swan-drawn boat, Paget designed a graceful swan to hide the boat captain. While today's swan boats are larger than the 1877 original, they still utilize the same technology and they are still managed by Paget's descendants.

Take a Breather in the Public Garden

★ **Top Tips**

○ Friends of the Public Garden (FPG) offers free walking tours from May to September. The one-hour tour departs from the *Make Way for Ducklings* statue. See the website for the schedule.

○ If you prefer a self-guided tour, look for the FPG app.

○ Don't feed the ducks or squirrels, no matter how hungry they look!

✕ **Take a Break**

Bistro du Midi (p100) occupies a lovely spot overlooking the Public Garden.

If you prefer to pack a picnic, visit the food trucks or the **Earl of Sandwich** (📞617-426-1395; www.earlofsandwichusa.com; 1b Charles St, Boston Common; sandwiches $6-10; ⏲11am-6pm; T Park St, Boylston) on the Boston Common.

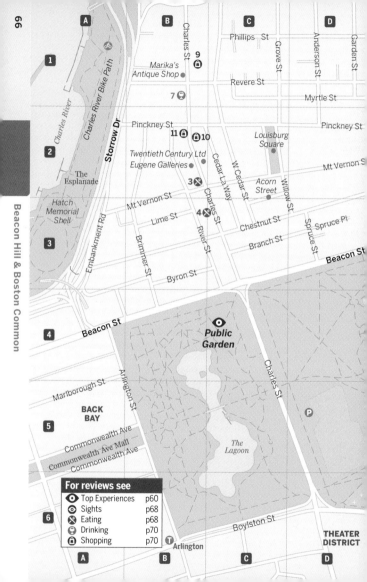

Beacon Hill & Boston Common

A
B
C
D

1

Charles St

Phillips St

Charles River Bike Path

Marika's
Antique Shop ●

9 🔒

Grove St

Anderson St

Garden St

Revere St

Myrtle St

7 🚌

2

Charles River

Storrow Dr

Pinckney St

Pinckney St

11 🔒 🔒 **10**

Louisburg
Square

The
Esplanade

Twentieth Century Ltd
Eugene Galleries ●

Cedar La Way

W Cedar St

Mt Vernon S

3

Hatch
Memorial
Shell

3 ✕

Acorn
Street ●

Willow St

Mt Vernon St

Charles St

Embankment Rd

Lime St

4 ✕

Chestnut St

Spruce Pl

Brimmer St

River St

Branch St

Spruce St

Beacon St

Byron St

4

Beacon St

👁
**Public
Garden**

Marlborough St

5

Arlington St

Charles St

BACK
BAY

Commonwealth Ave
Commonwealth Ave Mall
Commonwealth Ave

🅿

The
Lagoon

For reviews see
👁 Top Experiences p60
👁 Sights p68
✕ Eating p68
🍷 Drinking p70
🔒 Shopping p70

6

🚇 **Arlington**

Boylston St

THEATER
DISTRICT

A
B
C
D

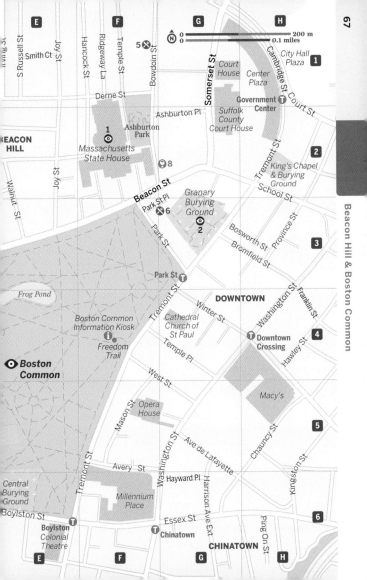

The Black Heritage Trail

Beacon Hill was never the exclusive domain of blue-blooded Brahmins. In the 19th century, freed African Americans settled on the back side of the hill and the neighborhood became a hive of activity focused on improving housing, establishing schools and creating opportunities for black residents. NPS rangers lead free tours of the **Black Heritage Trail** (p61).

The excellent, informative 90-minute guided tours exploring the history of the abolitionist movement and African American settlement on Beacon Hill. Tours depart from the Robert Gould Shaw memorial on the Boston Common. Alternatively, take a self-guided tour with the NPS Freedom Trail app (www.nps.gov/bost/planyourvisit/app.htm) or grab a route map from the Museum of African American History.

Sights

Massachusetts State House

NOTABLE BUILDING

1 ◉ MAP P66, F2

High atop Beacon Hill, Massachusetts' leaders and legislators attempt to turn their ideas into concrete policies and practices within the State House. John Hancock provided the land (previously part of his cow pasture) and Charles Bulfinch designed the commanding state capitol, but it was Oliver Wendell Holmes who called it 'the hub of the solar system' (thus earning Boston the nickname 'the Hub'). Free 40-minute tours cover the history, artwork, architecture and political personalities of the State House. (☏617-727-7030; www. sec.state.ma.us; cnr Beacon & Bowdoin Sts; admission free; ⏰8:45am-5pm Mon-Fri, tours 10am-3:30pm Mon-Fri; T Park St)

Granary Burying Ground

CEMETERY

2 ◉ MAP P66, G3

Dating from 1660, this atmospheric atoll is crammed with historic headstones, many with evocative (and creepy) carvings. This is the final resting place of favorite revolutionary heroes, including Paul Revere, Samuel Adams, John Hancock and James Otis. Benjamin Franklin is buried in Philadelphia, but the Franklin family plot contains his parents. (Tremont St; ⏰9am-5pm; T Park St)

Eating

Tatte

BAKERY $

3 🍴 MAP P66, B2

The aroma of buttery goodness – and the lines stretching out the door – signal your arrival at this fabulous bakery on the lower floor of the historic Charles St Meeting

House. Swoon-worthy pastries from $3 taste even more amazing if you're lucky enough to score a table on the sunny front patio. (☎617-723-5555; www.tattebakery.com; 70 Charles St; mains $10-14; ⏱7am-8pm Mon-Fri, from 8am Sat, 8am-7pm Sun; Ⓣ Charles/MGH)

Paramount   CAFETERIA $$

4 ⊗ MAP P66, B3

This old-fashioned cafeteria is a neighborhood favorite. A-plus diner fare includes pancakes, home fries, burgers and sandwiches, and hearty salads. Banana and caramel French toast is an obvious go-to for the brunch crowd. Don't sit down until you get your food! The wait may seem endless, but it is worth it. (☎617-720-1152; www.paramount boston.com; 44 Charles St; mains $17-

24; ⏱7am-10pm Mon-Fri, from 8am Sat & Sun; 🍴♿; Ⓣ Charles/MGH)

Grotto   ITALIAN $$

5 ⊗ MAP P66, F1

In a word: romantic. Tucked into a basement on the back side of Beacon Hill, this dark, cave-like place lives up to its name. The funky decor reflects the innovative menu. Reservations recommended. (☎617-227-3434; www.grottorestaurant.com; 37 Bowdoin St; mains $21-27, 3-course prix-fixe dinner $36-42; ⏱11:30am-3pm Mon-Fri, 5-10pm daily; Ⓣ Bowdoin)

No 9 Park   EUROPEAN $$$

6 ⊗ MAP P66, G3

This swanky place has been around since 1998, but it still tops

Granary Burying Ground

many fine-dining lists. Chef-owner Barbara Lynch has now cast her celebrity-chef spell all around town, but this is the place that made her famous. Delectable French and Italian culinary masterpieces and first-rate wine list. Reservations recommended. (📞617-742-9991; www.no9park.com; 9 Park St; mains $37-47, 6-course tasting menu $125; ⏲5-9pm Mon-Wed, to 10pm Thu-Sat, 4-8pm Sun; Ⓣ Park St)

Drinking

Pressed   JUICE BAR

7 📍 MAP P66, B1

We'll call it a juice bar, since it does make its own juices (out of every fruit and vegetable imaginable) as well as delicious vegan 'superfood shakes' ($10). But the 'toasts' and 'greens' also deserve mention. Both your body and your taste buds will thank you for eating and drinking this tasty, healthy fare. (📞857-350-3103; www.pressed boston.com; 120 Charles St; ⏲8am-6pm Mon-Fri, from 9am Sat & Sun; 📶 Ⓣ Charles/MGH)

21st Amendment   PUB

8 📍 MAP P66, G2

Named for one of the US Constitution's most important amendments – the one repealing Prohibition – this quintessential tavern is an ever-popular haunt for State House workers to meet up and talk about the wheels of government. The place feels especially cozy during winter, when you'll feel pretty good about yourself as you drink a stout near the copper-hooded fireplace. (📞617-227-7100; www.21stboston.com; 150 Bowdoin St; ⏲11:30am-2am; Ⓣ Park St)

Shopping

Paridaez   CLOTHING

9 🔒 MAP P66, B1

Boston designer Allison Daroie knows women play many roles, and she believes their clothing should too. That's why her classy, minimalist pieces can transform from daytime to evening, from dressy to casual, from conservative to flirtatious. These styles are so versatile, it's sometimes hard to say exactly what they are (like the ingenious Albatross 3-in-1 skirt+dress+tank). (📞617-835-5396; www.paridaez.com; 127 Charles St; ⏲noon-6pm; Ⓣ Charles/MGH)

Hidden Beacon Hill

Take a detour away from Charles St to discover a few Beacon Hill gems. There is no more pretigious address than **Louisburg Sq** (p73), a cluster of stately brick row houses facing a private park. Nearby, **Acorn St** (Map p66, C2; Ⓣ Charles/MGH) is Boston's narrowest street, a knobbly cobblestone alleyway that was once home to artisans and service people.

Antiquing on Beacon Hill

There was a time when Charles St was lined with antique shops and nothing else: some historians claim that the country's antique trade began right here on Beacon Hill. There are still enough antique shops to thrill the *Antiques Roadshow* lover in you.

Eugene Galleries (Map p66, B2; ☎ 617-227-3062; www.eugen-egalleries.com; 76 Charles St; ⏰11am-6pm Mon-Sat, from noon Sun; ⓣ Charles/MGH) This tiny shop has a remarkable selection of antique prints and maps, especially focusing on old Boston.

Twentieth Century Ltd (Map p66, B2; ☎ 617-742-1031; www.boston-vintagejewelry.com; 73 Charles St; ⏰11am-6pm Mon-Sat, noon-5pm Sun) Not just jewelry, but vintage jewelry, made by the great designers of yesteryear.

Marika's Antique Shop (Map p66, B1; ☎ 617-523-4520; 130 Charles St; ⏰10am-5pm Tue-Sat) A treasure trove of jewelry, silver and porcelain.

Beacon Hill Chocolates

FOOD & DRINKS

10 🅰 MAP P66, B2

This artisanal chocolatier puts equal effort into selecting fine chocolates from around the world and designing beautiful boxes to contain them. Using decoupage to affix old postcards, photos and illustrations, the boxes are works of art even before they are filled with truffles. Pick out an image of historic Boston as a souvenir for the sweet tooth in your life. (☎617-725-1900; www.beaconhillchocolates.com; 91 Charles St; ⏰11am-7pm Mon-Sat, to 5:30pm Sun; ⓣCharles/MGH)

Good

JEWELRY

11 🅰 MAP P66, B2

So many lovely things to look at, from exquisite custom-designed jewelry and attractive housewares to quirky baby gifts, chic scarves and handbags. It's hard to ascertain the common theme here, except the items are unique, stylish and supremely classy – and made in New England. Browsing is encouraged. (☎617-982-6777; www.shopatgood.com; 98 Charles St; ⏰10am-6pm Tue-Sat; ⓣCharles/MGH)

Walking Tour 🥾

Green Spaces & Shopping Places

Everybody knows about its world-class museums and historical sites, but Boston also offers a network of verdant parks, welcoming waterways and delightful shopping streets, making it a wonderful walking city. Take a break from the crowded downtown streets and discover another side of Boston.

Walk Facts

Start Boston Common; T Park St

Finish Boston Common

Length 2.5 miles; three hours

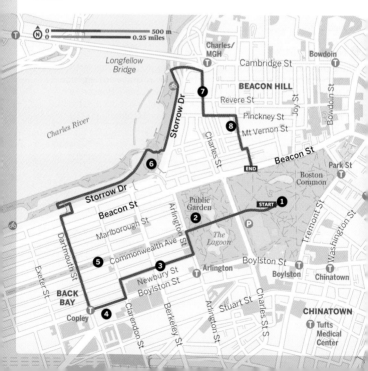

❶ Boston Common

Start at the **country's oldest public park** (p60), sprinkled with monuments and memorabilia. Follow busy Bostonians crisscrossing the Common and exit the park from the western side.

❷ Public Garden

The **Public Garden** (p64) is a 24-acre botanical oasis of Victorian flowerbeds, verdant grass and weeping willows shading a tranquil lagoon. At any time of year, don't miss the famous statue *Make Way for Ducklings*, based on the beloved children's book.

❸ Newbury Street

Exiting the Public Garden through its southwestern gate, stroll west on swanky Newbury St, perfect for window-shopping and people-watching.

❹ Copley Square

Boston's most exquisite architecture is clustered around this stately Back Bay plaza. The Romanesque **Trinity Church** (p108) is particularly lovely as reflected in the modern **John Hancock Tower** (p109). Opposite, the elegant neo-Renaissance **Boston Public Library** (p106) is packed with treasures.

❺ Commonwealth Avenue

Heading north, cross Commonwealth Ave, the grandest of Back Bay's grand avenues. Lined with brownstones and studded with 19th-century art, the 'Mall' offers an eclectic perspective on history.

❻ Charles River Esplanade

The southern bank of the Charles River Basin is known as the **Esplanade** (p112), an enticing urban escape with grassy knolls and cooling waterways designed by Frederick Law Olmsted. Walk northeast, enjoying the breezes and views of the river.

❼ Charles Street

Intriguing history, iconic architecture and unparalleled neighborhood charm make Beacon Hill one of Boston's most prestigious addresses. Traversing the flat of the hill, **Charles St** is an enchanting spot for browsing boutiques and haggling over antiques.

❽ Louisburg Square

Stroll down residential streets lit with gas lanterns, admire the distinguished brick town houses and discover streets such as stately **Louisburg Square** (Map p66, C2; T Charles/MGH) that capture the neighborhood's grandeur. Continue south to return to the Common.

Explore ◉
Downtown & Seaport District

Much of Boston's tourist activity takes place in this central neighborhood. Downtown is crammed with colonial buildings and harborside attractions, while the Seaport District attracts visitors with its dynamic contemporary-art museum and many waterfront dining options.

Short List

○ **Rose Kennedy Greenway (p81)** *Strolling, playing and admiring art along Boston's linear park.*

○ **Whale Watching (p83)** *Spying on whales, dolphins and other sea life.*

○ **Boston Massacre Site (p80)** *Finding the plaque that marks the spot of the first violent confrontation of the American Revolution.*

○ **Institute of Contemporary Art (p76)** *Contemplating the artistic curiosities and admiring the stunning harbor and city views.*

○ **Boston Tea Party Ships (p80)** *Boarding replicas of the historic ships and tossing tea crates into the harbor.*

Getting There & Around

Ⓜ For Faneuil Hall, take the T to Haymarket, Government Center or State. The Aquarium stop offers the easiest access to the waterfront.

⚓ City Water Taxi stops at Long Wharf on the waterfront.

🚌 Connected to the metro system, the silver-line bus (SL1 or SL2) travels from South Station through the Seaport District.

Neighborhood Map on p78

Boston Tea Party Ships & Museum (p80)

Top Experience 📷
Experience the New at the ICA

Boston has become a focal point for contemporary art in the 21st century, as hundreds of thousands of visitors flock to the dramatic quarters of the Institute of Contemporary Art (ICA). In addition to its innovative collections, the spacious, light-filled interior hosts multimedia presentations, educational programs and studio space.

◉ MAP P78, G4

📞 617-478-3100

www.icaboston.org

25 Harbor Shore Dr

adult/child $15/free, Thu 5-9pm free

🕙 10am-5pm Tue, Wed, Sat & Sun, to 9pm Thu & Fri

🚌 SL1, SL2, Ⓣ South Station

Founders Gallery

Arguably, the ICA building and setting are as much of an attraction as the art. Opened in 2006, the structure skillfully incorporates its surroundings into the architecture. In the Founders Gallery, which spans the entire width of the building, a glass wall virtually eliminates any barrier between viewer and seascape.

Permanent Collection

In addition to dynamic temporary exhibits, the ICA showcases national and international artists in its permanent collection. You'll find the likes of graffiti artist Shepard Fairey, conceptual artist Gillian Wearing, video artist Christian Jankowski, photographer Boris Mikhailov and sculptor Sarah Sze. Look for all manner of art, from painting to video to multidimensional mixed-media mash-ups.

Mediatheque

The Mediatheque is the museum's digital media center, where visitors can use the computer stations to learn more about featured art and artists. The terraced room has a wall of windows at the front, but the room's unique downward-slanting perspective shows only the dancing and rippling of water, with no horizon in sight.

Foundation Theater

The Barbara Lee Family Foundation Theater is one of the ICA's coolest features. With a wooden floor and ceiling and glass walls, the two-story venue is an extension of the boardwalk outside. It's a remarkable backdrop for edgy theater, dance, music and performance art.

★ Top Tips

o Take advantage of the ICA audio commentary that is available free with admission. Borrow an iPod from the front desk or download the tracks to your own device from the museum website.

o The ICA offers guided highlights tours on Saturday and Sunday (1pm and 2:30pm) and Thursday evenings (6pm and 7pm).

o Admission is free for all on Thursdays after 5pm.

o Admission is always free for kids aged under 17.

✗ Take a Break

The ICA cafe was closed for renovation at the time of research, and is due to reopen in late 2019.

For great seafood and drinks with a buzzy atmosphere, walk half a mile west along the waterfront to the Barking Crab (p85).

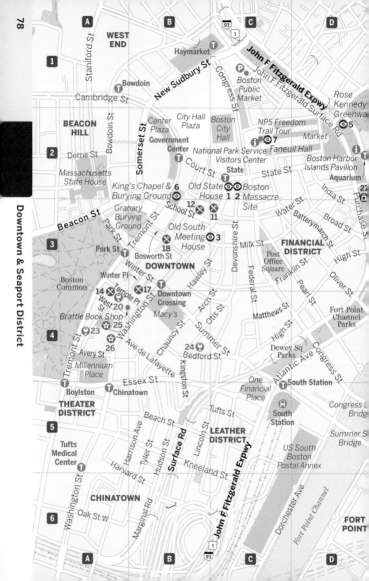

Downtown & Seaport District

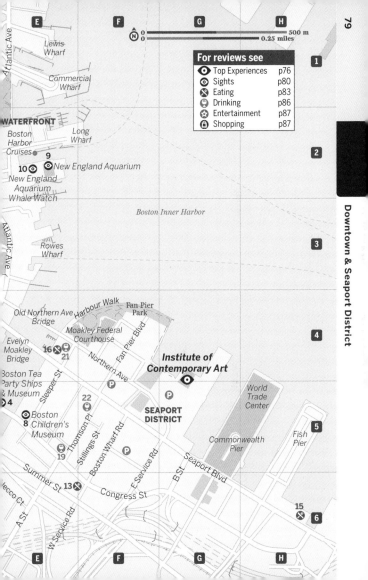

For reviews see

◉ Top Experiences	p76
◉ Sights	p80
✪ Eating	p83
⊙ Drinking	p86
✪ Entertainment	p87
🔒 Shopping	p87

0   500 m
0   0.25 miles

E **F** **G** **H**

Atlantic Ave

Lewis Wharf

Commercial Wharf

WATERFRONT

Boston Harbor Cruises

9

10 ◉ ◉ New England Aquarium

New England Aquarium Whale Watch

Long Wharf

Atlantic Ave

Boston Inner Harbor

Rowes Wharf

Old Northern Ave Bridge

Harbour Walk

Fan Pier Park

Moakley Federal Courthouse

Evelyn Moakley Bridge

16 ✪ 21

Northern Ave

Fan Pier Blvd

Institute of Contemporary Art ◉

World Trade Center

Boston Tea Party Ships & Museum

◉ 4

Sleeper St

22

SEAPORT DISTRICT

Commonwealth Pier

Fish Pier

◉ Boston Children's Museum

8

19

Thomson Pl

Stillings St

Boston Wharf Rd

E-Service Rd

B St

Seaport Blvd

Summer St

13 ✪

Congress St

Mecco Ct

W Service Rd

A St

15 ✪

E **F** **G** **H**

Downtown & Seaport District

Sights

Old State House HISTORIC BUILDING

1 ◉ MAP P78, C2

Dating from 1713, the Old State House is Boston's oldest surviving public building, where the Massachusetts Assembly used to debate the issues of the day before the Revolution. The building is best known for its balcony, where the Declaration of Independence was first read to Bostonians in 1776. Inside, the Old State House contains a small museum of revolutionary memorabilia, with videos and multimedia presentations about the Boston Massacre, which took place out front. (☏617-720-1713; www.bostonhistory.org; 206 Washington St; adult/child $10/free; ⊙9am-6pm Jun-Aug, to 5pm Sep-May; ⊤State)

Boston Massacre Site MONUMENT

2 ◉ MAP P78, C2

Directly in front of the Old State House, encircled by cobblestones, a bronze plaque marks the spot where the first blood was shed for the American independence movement. On March 5, 1770, an angry mob of colonists swarmed the British soldiers guarding the State House, hurling snowballs, rocks and insults. Thus provoked, the soldiers fired into the crowd and killed five townspeople, including Crispus Attucks, a former slave. The incident sparked enormous anti-British sentiment. (cnr State & Devonshire Sts; ⊤State)

Old South Meeting House HISTORIC BUILDING

3 ◉ MAP P78, C3

'No tax on tea!' That was the decision on December 16, 1773, when 5000 angry colonists gathered here to protest British taxes, leading to the Boston Tea Party. Download an audio of the historic pre–Tea Party meeting from the museum website, then visit the graceful meeting house to check out the exhibit on the history of the building and the protest. (☏617-482-6439; www.osmh.org; 310 Washington St; adult/child $6/1; ⊙9:30am-5pm Apr-Oct, 10am-4pm Nov-Mar; ⊕; ⊤Downtown Crossing, State)

Boston Tea Party Ships & Museum MUSEUM

4 ◉ MAP P78, E5

'Boston Harbor a teapot tonight!' To protest against unfair taxes, a gang of rebellious colonists dumped 342 chests of tea into the water. The 1773 protest – the Boston Tea Party – set into motion the events leading to the Revolutionary War. Nowadays, replica Tea Party Ships are moored at Griffin's Wharf, alongside an excellent experiential museum dedicated to the catalytic event. Using re-enactments, multimedia and fun exhibits, the museum addresses all aspects of the Boston Tea Party and subsequent events. (☏866-955-0667; www.bostonteapartyship.com; Congress St Bridge; adult/child $30/18; ⊙10am-5pm; ⊕; ⊤South Station)

Rose Kennedy Greenway

PARK

5 ◎ MAP P78, D2

Where once was a hulking overhead highway, now winds a 27-acre strip of landscaped gardens, fountain-lined greens and public art installations. The park has something for everyone: the artist-driven Greenway Open Market (p87) for weekend shoppers, food trucks for weekday lunchers, summertime block parties for music lovers and **Trillium Garden** (📞857-449-0083; www. trilliumbrewing.com; cnr Atlantic Ave & High St; ⊙2-10pm Wed-Fri, from 11am Sat, 1-8pm Sun May-Oct; 🛜; T South Station, Aquarium) for beer drinkers. Cool off in the whimsical **Rings Fountain**, walk the calming **laby-rinth** (♿; T Haymarket), or take a ride on the custom-designed **Greenway Carousel** (per ride $3; ⊙11am-7pm Apr-Dec; ♿). (📞617-292-0020; www.rosekennedygreenway. org; ♿; T Aquarium, Haymarket)

King's Chapel & Burying Ground

CHURCH, CEMETERY

6 ◎ MAP P78, B2

Puritan Bostonians were not pleased when the original Anglican church was erected on this site in 1688. The granite chapel standing today – built in 1754 – houses the largest bell ever made by Paul Revere, as well as a historic organ. The adjacent burying ground is the oldest in the city. Besides the biweekly services, recitals are

Old South Meeting House

BORISVETSHEV/SHUTTERSTOCK ©

held here every week (12:15pm Tuesday). (📞617-523-1749; www.kings-chapel.org; 58 Tremont St; donation $3, tours adult/child $7/3; ⏰church 10am-4:30pm Mon-Sat, 1:30-5pm Sun, hourly tours 10am-3pm; 🚇Government Center)

Faneuil Hall
HISTORIC BUILDING

7 ◉ MAP P78, C2

'Those who cannot bear free speech had best go home,' said Wendell Phillips. 'Faneuil Hall is no place for slavish hearts.' Indeed, this public meeting place was the site of so much rabble-rousing that it earned the nickname the 'Cradle of Liberty.' After the revolution, Faneuil Hall was a forum for meetings about abolition, women's suffrage and war. You can hear about the building's history from National Park Service rangers in the historic hall on the 2nd floor. (📞617-242-5642; www.nps.gov/bost; Congress St; admission free; ⏰9am-5pm; 🚇State, Haymarket, Government Center)

Boston Children's Museum
MUSEUM

8 ◉ MAP P78, E5

The interactive educational exhibits at the delightful Boston Children's Museum keep kids entertained for hours. Highlights include a bubble exhibit, rock-climbing walls, a hands-on construction site and intercultural immersion experiences. The light-filled atrium features an amazing three-story climbing maze. (📞617-426-6500; www.bostonchildrens museum.org; 308 Congress St; $17, Fri 5-9pm $1; ⏰10am-5pm Sat-Thu, to 9pm Fri; 🚼; 🚇South Station)

Columbia Point

Columbia Point juts into the harbor south of the city center in Dorchester. Take the red line to JFK/UMass and catch a free shuttle bus (departures every 20 minutes).

John F Kennedy Presidential Library & Museum (📞617-514-1600; www.jfklibrary.org; Columbia Point; adult/child $14/10; ⏰9am-5pm; 🚇JFK/UMass) The official memorial to the 35th president – a striking, modern, marble building designed by IM Pei. The museum is a fitting tribute to JFK's life and legacy.

Edward M Kennedy Institute for the US Senate (EMK Institute; 📞617-740-7000; www.emkinstitute.org; Columbia Point; adult/child $16/8; ⏰10am-5pm Tue-Sun; 🚇JKF/UMass) The state-of-the-art facility uses advanced technology, multimedia exhibits and interactive designs to engage visitors and demonstrate the functioning (and sometimes non-functioning) of the legislative process.

New England Aquarium

AQUARIUM

9 ⊙ MAP P78, E2

Teeming with sea creatures of all sizes, shapes and colors, this giant fishbowl is the centerpiece of downtown Boston's waterfront. The main attraction is the three-story Giant Ocean Tank, which swirls with thousands of creatures great and small, including turtles, sharks and eels. Countless side exhibits explore the lives and habitats of other underwater oddities, as well as penguins and marine mammals. (📞617-973-5200; www.neaq. org; Central Wharf; adult/child $27/19; ⊙9am-5pm Mon-Fri, to 6pm Sat & Sun, 1hr later Jul & Aug; 🅿 👫; 🎫 Aquarium)

New England Aquarium Whale Watch

WHALE WATCHING

10 ⊙ MAP P78, E2

Set off from Long Wharf for the journey to Stellwagen Bank, a rich feeding ground for whales, dolphins and marine birds. Keen-eyed boat captains and onboard naturalists can answer all your questions and have been trained by New England Aquarium experts to ensure that the tours do not interfere with the animals or harm them in any way. (📞617-227-4321; www.neaq.org/exhibits/whale-watch; Central Wharf; adult/child/infant $53/33/16; ⊙times vary late Mar–mid-Nov; 🎫 Aquarium)

Eating

Spyce

INTERNATIONAL $

11 🍴 MAP P78, C3

A new concept in dining, Spyce is the brainchild of four hungry MIT graduates, who teamed up with a Michelin-starred chef. The food is all prepared in a robotic kitchen – that is, self-rotating woks that are programmed for both the optimal temperature and time to create consistently perfect 'bowls' of goodness. It's fast, fresh, healthy and pretty darn delicious. It's also vegetarian, vegan or gluten-free, if you wish. (www.spyce.com; 241 Washington St; bowls $7.50; ⊙10:30am-10pm; 🍴👫; 🎫 State)

Clover DTX

VEGETARIAN $

12 🍴 MAP P78, B3

Right on the Freedom Trail of Boston, the first downtown branch of this socially conscious local success story serves vegetarian treats morning, noon and night, from breakfast sandwiches and bowls in the morning to platters of BBQ seitan or chickpea fritters the rest of the day. The restaurant also offers a range of interesting sodas and teas.(www.cloverfoodlab. com; 27 School St; mains $8-12; ⊙7am-9pm Mon-Fri, 8am-8pm Sat-Sun; 🍴; 🎫 State)

Row 34

SEAFOOD $$

13 🍴 MAP P78, E6

In the heart of the new Seaport District, set in a sharp, postindustrial space, this place offers a dozen types of raw oysters and clams, alongside an amazing selection of craft beers. There's also a full menu of cooked seafood, ranging from the traditional to the trendy. (📞617-553-5900; www.row34.com; 383 Congress St; oysters $2-3, mains $14-32; ⏱11:30am-10pm Sun-Thu, to 11pm Fri & Sat; Ⓣ South Station)

Boston Public Market

🍽

A locavore's longtime dream-come-true, this daily farmers **market** (BPM; Map p78, C1; 📞617-973-4909; www.bostonpublicmarket.org; 136 Blackstone St; ⏱8am-8pm Mon-Sat, 10am-6pm Sun; 📶; Ⓣ Haymarket) gives shoppers access to fresh foodstuffs, grown, harvested and produced right here in New England. Come for seasonal produce, fresh seafood, meats and poultry from local farms, artisan cheeses and dairy products, maple syrup and other sweets. Don't miss the local brews found in Hopsters' Alley. Reserve your spot for a free one-hour tour (10am and 11am, Thursday and Friday).

jm Curley

PUB FOOD $$

14 🍴 MAP P78, A4

This dim but inviting bar is a perfect place to settle in for a Dark & Stormy on a dark and stormy night. The fare is bar food like you've never had before: Curley's cracka jack (caramel corn with bacon); mac 'n' cheese (served in a cast-iron skillet); and fried pickles (yes, you read that right). That's why they call it a gastropub. The place is named for Boston's beloved four-term (including one term - his last - that he served from prison) mayor. (📞617-338-5333; www.jmcurleyboston.com; 21 Temple Pl; mains $10-20; ⏱11:30am-1am Mon-Sat, to 10pm Sunday; 🍴; Ⓣ Downtown Crossing)

Legal Harborside

SEAFOOD $$

15 🍴 MAP P78, H6

This vast glass-fronted waterfront complex offers three different restaurant concepts on three floors. Our favorite is the 1st floor – a casual restaurant and fish market that is a throwback to Legal's original outlet from 1904. The updated menu includes a raw bar, small plates, seafood grills and plenty of international influences. (📞617-477-2900; www.legalseafoods.com; 270 Northern Ave; mains $18-30; ⏱11am-10pm Sun-Thu, to 11pm Fri & Sat; 🚌SL1, SL2, Ⓣ South Station)

Barking Crab

SEAFOOD $$

16  MAP P78, E4

Big buckets of crabs (snow, king, Dungeness etc), steamers dripping in lemon and butter, paper plates piled high with all things fried, pitchers of ice-cold beer... Devour your feast at communal picnic tables overlooking the water. Service is slack, noise levels are high, but the atmosphere is jovial. Prepare to wait for a table if the weather is warm. (617-426-2722; www.barkingcrab.com; 88 Sleeper St; sandwiches $14-18, mains $18-36; 11:30am-10pm Sun-Wed, to 11pm Thu-Sat; SL1, SL2, South Station)

Yvonne's

MODERN AMERICAN $$$

17 MAP P78, B3

Upon arrival at Yvonne's, staff will usher you discreetly through closed doors into a hidden 'modern supper club.' The spectacular space artfully blends old-school luxury with contemporary eclecticism. The menu of mostly small plates does the same, with items from tuna crudo to baked oysters to chicken and quinoa meatballs. (617-267-0047; www.yvonnesboston.com; 2 Winter Pl; 5-11pm, bar to 2am; Park)

Marliave

FRENCH $$$

18 MAP P78, B3

Dating to 1885, the Marliave has all of its vintage architectural quirks still intact, from the mosaic floor to

Barking Crab

the tin ceilings. The wide-ranging menu includes quirky cocktails, a raw bar, delicious egg dishes, home-made pasta and old-fashioned Sunday dinners. (📞617-422-0004; www.marliave.com; 10 Bosworth St; mains $18-38; ⏰11am-10pm; 🍴; T Park St)

Drinking

Drink
COCKTAIL BAR

19 🚇 MAP P78, E5

There is no cocktail menu at Drink. Instead you have a chat with the bartender, and he or she will whip something up according to your mood and taste. It takes seriously the art of mixology – and you will too, after you sample one of its concoctions. The subterranean space, with its low-lit, sexy ambience, makes a great date destination. (📞617-695-1806; www.drinkfortpoint.

Brattle Book Shop

Since 1825, the **Brattle Book Shop** (Map p78, A4; 📞617-542-0210; www.brattlebookshop.com; 9 West St; ⏰9am-5:30pm Mon-Sat; T Park St, Downtown Crossing) has catered to Boston's literati: it's a treasure trove crammed with out-of-print, rare and 1st edition books. Ken Gloss – whose family has owned this gem since 1949 – is an expert on antiquarian books, moonlighting as a consultant and appraiser.

com; 348 Congress St; ⏰4pm-1am; 🚉SL1, SL2, T South Station)

Democracy Brewing
BREWERY

20 🚇 MAP P78, A4

The beer is fresh, the fries are crispy perfection and the politics are 'woke.' Not only do they brew exceptional beer at Democracy Brewing, they also ferment revolution – by supporting democratic businesses and organizing community events. (📞857-263-8604; www.democracybrewing.com; 35 Temple Pl; ⏰11:30am-11pm Sun-Thu, to 1am Fri & Sat; T Downtown Crossing)

Lookout Rooftop Bar
BAR

21 🚇 MAP P78, E4

This trendy bar starts filling up almost as soon as it opens, as hotel guests and local workers ascend to the rooftop to take in potent drinks and spectacular views. When temperatures drop, there are heaters and igloos to keep you warm. Note the dress code. (📞617-338-3030; www.theenvoyhotel.com; Envoy Hotel, 70 Sleeper St; ⏰4-11pm Mon-Thu, to midnight Fri & Sat, from noon Sun; 🚉SL1, SL2, T South Station)

Trillium Fort Point
MICROBREWERY

22 🚇 MAP P78, F5

Trillium has been brewing beer in the Fort Point area for years. But it was only recently that they opened this fantastic tap room, complete with bar, dining room and rooftop deck. Enjoy the full range of Trillium favorites – not only India pale ales, but also American pale ales, gose ales, wild ales and stouts. (☎857-449-0083; www.trilliumbrewing.com; 50 Thompson Pl; ⏰11am-11pm; Ⓣ South Station)

Thinking Cup   CAFE
23 🚇 MAP P78, A4

There are a few things that make the Thinking Cup special. One is the French hot chocolate – *ooh la la*. Another is the Stumptown Coffee, the Portland brew that has earned accolades from coffee drinkers around the country. (☎617-482-5555; www.thinkingcup.com; 165 Tremont St; ⏰7am-10pm Mon-Wed, to 11pm Thu-Sun; Ⓣ Boylston)

Good Life   CLUB
24 🚇 MAP P78, B4

The Good Life means a lot of things to a lot of people – solid lunch option, after-work hangout, trivia-night place etc. But the top reason to come here is to get your groove on. There are three bars and two dance floors, with great DJs spinning tunes Thursday to Saturday. (☎617-451-2622; www.goodlifebar.com; 28 Kingston St; ⏰11am-11pm Mon-Wed, to 2am Thu-Sat; Ⓣ Downtown Crossing)

Entertainment

Opera House   LIVE PERFORMANCE
25 ⭐ MAP P78, A4

This lavish theater has been restored to its 1928 glory, complete with mural-painted ceiling, gilded molding and plush velvet curtains. The glitzy venue regularly hosts productions from the Broadway Across America series, and is also the main performance space for the **Boston Ballet** (www.bostonballet.org). (☎800-982-2787; www.bostonoperahouse.com; 539 Washington St; Ⓣ Downtown Crossing)

Paramount Center   THEATER
26 ⭐ MAP P78, A4

This art deco masterpiece, restored by Emerson College, re-opened in 2010. Originally a 1700-seat, single-screen cinema, it was owned by Paramount Pictures. The facility includes a cinema and a black-box stage, as well as the more traditional but still grand main stage. (☎617-824-8400; www.paramountboston.org; 559 Washington St; Ⓣ Chinatown, Downtown Crossing)

Shopping

Greenway Open Market   ARTS & CRAFTS
27 🔒 MAP P78, D2

This weekend artist market brings out dozens of vendors to display their wares in the open air. Look for unique, handmade gifts, jewelry, bags, paintings, ceramics and other arts and crafts – most of which are locally and ethically made. Food trucks are always on hand to cater to the hungry. (☎800-401-6557; www.newenglandopenmarkets.com; Rose Kennedy Greenway; ⏰11am-5pm Sat, plus 1st & 3rd Sun May-Oct; 🛜; Ⓣ Aquarium)

Worth a Trip 🔭

Hop Around Boston Harbor Islands

Boston Harbor is sprinkled with 34 islands, many of which are open for trail walking, bird-watching, fishing, swimming and camping. The islands offer a range of ecosystems – sandy beaches, rocky cliffs, fresh- and saltwater marshes, and forested trails – only 45 minutes from downtown Boston. Since the massive, multi-million-dollar cleanup of Boston Harbor in the mid-1990s, the islands have become one of the city's most magnificent natural assets.

Getting There

🚢 Boston Harbor Cruises offers seasonal ferry services from Long Wharf to Georges Island or Spectacle Island (adult/child $20/13), from where you catch other boats to the smaller islands.

Boston Harbor Islands Pavilion

Ideally located on the Rose Kennedy Greenway, this **information center** (Map p78, D2; ☎617-223-8666; www.bostonharborislands.org; cnr State St & Atlantic Ave; ☉9am-4:30pm mid-May–Jun & Sep-early Oct, to 6pm Jul & Aug; 🛜; Ⓣ Aquarium) will tell you everything you need to know to plan your visit to the **Boston Harbor Islands** (☉9am-dusk mid-Apr–mid-Oct).

Georges Island

Georges Island is one of the transportation hubs for the Boston Harbor Islands. It is also the site of Fort Warren, a 19th-century fort and Civil War prison. While National Park Service (NPS) rangers give guided tours of the fort and there is a small museum, it is largely abandoned, with many dark tunnels, creepy corners and magnificent lookouts to discover.

Spectacle Island

A Harbor Islands hub, Spectacle Island (pictured) has a large marina, a solar-powered visitor center, a healthy snack bar and sandy, supervised beaches. Five miles of walking trails provide access to a 157ft peak overlooking the harbor.

Lovells Island

With camping and picnicking facilities, Lovells is one of the most popular Harbor Islands destinations. Two deadly shipwrecks may bode badly for seafarers, but that doesn't seem to stop recreational boaters, swimmers and sunbathers from lounging on Lovells' long rocky beach.

Bumpkin Island

The beaches on Bumpkin are not the best for swimming, as they are slate and seashell, but a network of trails leads through fields overgrown

★ **Top Tips**

∘ Don't try to visit more than two islands in one day; you'll end up spending all your time riding on or waiting for boats.

∘ Check the website for special events, such as live music, outdoor activities and other family programs, especially on Georges and Spectacle Islands.

✕ **Take a Break**

On Georges and Spectacle Islands, there are surprisingly good grills run by **Salty's** (www.saltwaterboston.com/saltys; mains $7-10; ☉variable). There is no food or water on the other islands, so pack a picnic.

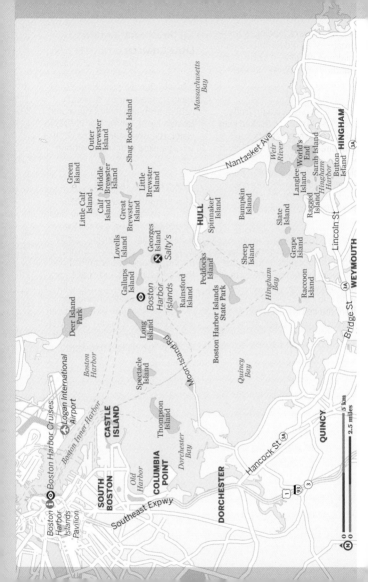

with wildflowers, leading to the remains of an old farmhouse and a children's hospital. It's one of four islands with camping facilities.

Grape Island

Grape Island is rich with fruity goodness. An arbor decked with cultivated grapes greets you opposite the boat dock, while the wild raspberries, bayberries and elderberries growing along the island's scrubby wooded trails attract abundant birdlife. The island also offers a few campsites.

Peddocks Island

One of the largest Harbor Islands, Peddocks consists of four headlands connected by sandbars. Hiking trails wander through marsh, pond and coastal environs, and there are campsites and yurts if you wish to spend the night.

Little Brewster Island

Little Brewster (☎ 617-223-8666; www.bostonharborislands.org/boston light; adult/child $35/25; ⏱ 9:30am & 1pm Fri-Sun Jun-Sep; 🚤 from Long Wharf) is the country's oldest light station and site of the iconic Boston Light, dating from 1783. To visit Little Brewster, you must take an organized tour (reservations required).

Thompson Island

Thompson Island (☎ 617-328-3900; www.thompsonisland.org; adult/child $17/10; ⏱ 8am-4:30pm Sat & Sun Jun-Aug; 🚤 from EDIC Pier) is privately owned by Outward Bound, a nonprofit organization that develops fun and challenging physical adventures, especially for training and developing leadership skills. As such, the public can explore its 200-plus acres only on weekends, when it's wonderful for walking, fishing and birding.

Explore ◉
South End & Chinatown

Chinatown, Theater District and the Leather District are overlapping areas filled with glitzy theaters, Chinese restaurants and the remnants of Boston's shoe and leather industry (now converted lofts and clubs). Nearby, the Victorian manses in the South End have been reclaimed by artists and the LGBTIQ+ community, who have created a vibrant restaurant and gallery scene.

Short List

○ **Underground at Ink Block (p98)** Checking out the fantastic street art at Boston's latest postindustrial playground.

○ **Gourmet Dumpling House (p99)** Hitting Chinatown for pork buns, dumplings or dim sum delights.

○ **SoWa Open Market (p102)** Splurging on locally made creations, followed by Sunday brunch.

○ **Wally's Café (p101)** Packing into this cafe for old-time jazz and blues.

○ **SoWa Artists Guild (p98)** Popping into galleries and studios to peruse the art and hobnob with the artists on the first Friday of the month.

Getting There & Around

Ⓜ For the South End, take the orange line to Back Bay station or Tufts Medical Center station. Chinatown is served by its eponymous station. The green line Boylston station is handy for the Theater District.

🚍 For the South End the silver line bus runs down Washington St from South Station (SL4) or Downtown Crossing (SL5).

Neighborhood Map on p96

Chinatown Gate (p98) F11PHOTO/SHUTTERSTOCK ©

Walking Tour 🚶

South End Art Stroll

Boston's main art district is the South End. The artistic community has moved into the once-barren area south of Washington St (now known as SoWa), converting old warehouses into studios and galleries. For best results, do this walk on a summer Sunday (May to October) or in the evening on the first Friday of the month (year-round).

Walk Facts

Start Underground at Ink Block; [T] Tufts Medical Center

Finish Boston Center for the Arts; [T] Back Bay

Length 1 mile; 30 to 60 minutes

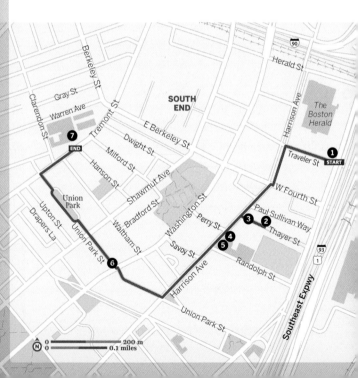

❶ Underground at Ink Block

The newest and edgiest art space in SoWa is **Underground at Ink Block** (p98), a showcase for the city's boldest and brightest street art. Very gritty, very city.

❷ SoWa Artists Guild

This is the epicenter of the South End art scene, where artists have carved out studios and gallery space from the former warehouses and factories on Harrison Ave. The **SoWa Artists Guild** (p98) hosts an Open Studios event on the first Friday of every month, and in summer the neighborhood streets fill with food trucks, a beer garden and markets selling art, vintage apparel and fresh produce.

❸ Thayer Street

There are dozens of venues lining the pedestrianized street between the former warehouses at 450 and 460 Harrison Ave. **Bromfield Art Gallery** (☎617-451-3605; www.bromfieldgallery.com; 450 Harrison Ave; admission free; ⊙noon-5pm Wed-Sun; 🚌SL4, SL5, 🚇Tufts Medical Center) for example, is a long-established artist-run gallery that features New England artists.

❹ Boston Sculptors Gallery

Peek into this unusual cooperative **gallery** (☎617-482-7781; www.bostonsculptors.com; 486 Harrison Ave; admission free; ⊙noon-6pm Wed-Sun; 🚌SL4, SL5, 🚇Tufts Medical Center), which has been going strong for more than 25 years. Three dozen local artists run the innovative gallery, dedicated to three-dimensional art in all media.

❺ Ars Libri

Ring the doorbell: **Ars Libri** (☎617-357-5212; www.arslibri.com; 500 Harrison Ave; ⊙9am-6pm Mon-Fri, 11am-5pm Sat; 🚌SL4, SL5, 🚇Tufts Medical Center) is an art bookstore extraordinaire, specializing in rare and out-of-print books. The former warehouse is filled from floor to ceiling with books on all aspects and eras of art, architecture and design. If you love books, and especially books about art, you'll love Ars Libri.

❻ Union Park Street

Turn up Union Park St to get a glimpse of the neighborhood's charming Victorian rowhouses, clustered around a tree-lined, fountain-filled park. This is South End architecture at its best.

❼ Boston Center for the Arts

Finish your walk at the Boston Center for the Arts, home of the **Mills Gallery** (☎617-426-5000; www.bcaonline.org; 551 Tremont St; admission free; ⊙noon-5pm Wed & Sun, to 9pm Thu-Sat; 🚇Back Bay), which hosts cutting-edge visual arts exhibits, and artist and curator talks. Exhibits feature established and emerging artists from Boston and around the country. Housed in the same complex are several performing arts venues.

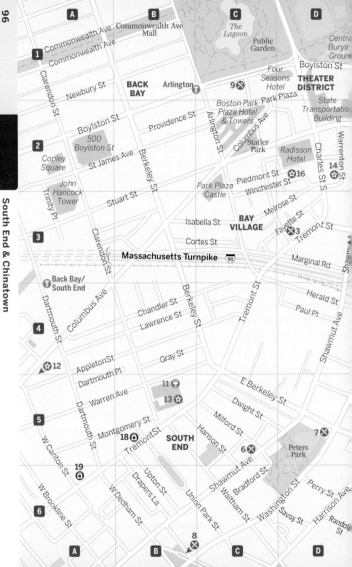

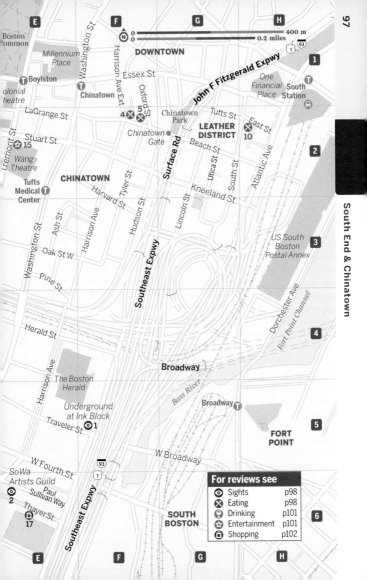

South End & Chinatown

E **F** **G** **H**

Boston
Common

Millennium
Place

T Boylston

Colonial
Theatre

T Chinatown

LaGrange St

1

DOWNTOWN

Washington St

Harrison Ave Ext

Essex St

Oxford St

John F Fitzgerald Expwy

One
Financial
Place

T South
Station

2

Stuart St

15

Tremont St

Wang
Theatre

Tufts
Medical
Center **T**

CHINATOWN

Washington St

Ash St

Oak St W

Pine St

Herald St

Harrison Ave

Harrison Ave

Tyler St

Hudson St

Harvard St

4 **5**

Chinatown
Gate

Chinatown
Park

LEATHER
DISTRICT

Tufts St

East St

10

Beach St

Utica St

Kneeland St

Surface Rd

Lincoln St

Southeast Expwy

South St

Atlantic Ave

US South
Boston
Postal Annex

2

3

Dorchester Ave

Fort Point Channel

4

The Boston
Herald

Underground
at Ink Block

Traveler St **1**

Broadway

Bass River

Broadway **T**

W Broadway

FORT
POINT

5

SoWa
Artists Guild

2

Paul
Sullivan Way

Thayer St

17

W Fourth St

Southeast Expwy

SOUTH
BOSTON

6

400 m

0.2 miles

For reviews see	
⊙ Sights	p98
✕ Eating	p98
🍷 Drinking	p101
✿ Entertainment	p101
🔒 Shopping	p102

E **F** **G** **H**

Chinatown Gate

The official entrance to Chinatown is the decorative **Chinatown Gate** (Map p96, G2; Beach St; T Chinatown), a gift from the city of Taipei. It is symbolic – not only as an entryway for guests visiting Chinatown, but also as an entryway for immigrants who are still settling here.

Surrounding the gate and anchoring the southern end of the Rose Kennedy Greenway is **Chinatown Park**. The plaza is often populated by local residents engaged in Xiangqi (Chinese chess) and Falun Gong (a Chinese spiritual practice).

Sights

Underground at Ink Block
PUBLIC ART

1 ◎ MAP P96, F5

What used to be an abandoned parking lot beneath the interstate is now an 8-acre playground and art space. The main draw is the fantastic mural project, which turned 150,000 sq ft of concrete wall space into a fabulous outdoor gallery for street art, with bold colorful pieces by a dozen local and national artists. To say the mural brightens the place up is an understatement. There's also a dog park, walking paths and fitness classes to get you moving. (www.undergroundinkblock.com; 90 Traveler St; ◷ 24hr; T Tufts Medical Center)

SoWa Artists Guild
GALLERY

2 ◎ MAP P96, E6

The brick-and-beam buildings along Harrison Ave were originally used to manufacture goods ranging from canned food to pianos. Now these factories turn out paintings and sculptures instead. Housing about 70 artist studios and more than a dozen galleries, the SoWa Artists Guild is the epicenter of the South End art district. There is a SoWa Open Studios event on the first Friday of every month, while many artists also welcome visitors on Sundays (p102). (☎ 857-362-7692; www.sowaartistsguild.com; 450 Harrison Ave; admission free; ◷ 5-9pm 1st Fri of month; 🚌 SL4, SL5, T Tufts Medical Center)

Eating

Mike & Patty's
SANDWICHES $

3 ✕ MAP P96, D3

Tucked away in Bay Village, this hole-in-the-wall gem of a corner sandwich shop does amazing things between two slices of bread. There are only eight options and they're all pretty perfect, but the hands-down favorite is the Breakfast Grilled Crack (fried egg, bacon and four kinds of cheese on sourdough). There's always a line but it moves quickly. No seating.

(☎617-423-3447; www.mikeandpattys.com; 12 Church St; sandwiches $9-12; ⏱8am-2pm; 🖋; T Tufts Medical Center, Arlington)

Avana Sushi

SUSHI $

4 ❌ MAP P96, F2

This place is essentially unmarked from the street, tucked into a tiny, cramped food court, sharing the space with a few other takeout places. There's only a handful of seats, but the sushi is fresh and affordable, and service is personable. It's hard to beat. We also appreciate the Styrofoam artwork, offering a commentary on our disposable culture, perhaps? (☎617-818-7782; www.avanasushi.com; 42 Beach St; sushi & sashimi $4-6; ⏱11am-10pm; T Chinatown)

Gourmet Dumpling House

CHINESE $

5 ❌ MAP P96, F2

Xiao long bao. That's all the Chinese you need to know to take advantage of the specialty at the Gourmet Dumpling House (or GDH, as it is fondly called). They are Shanghai soup dumplings, and they are fresh, doughy and delicious. The menu offers plenty of other options, including scrumptious crispy scallion pancakes. Come early or be prepared to wait (and yes, it's worth waiting if you arrive late). (☎617-338-6223; www.gourmetdumplinghouse.com; 52 Beach St; dumplings $5-8, mains $9-17; ⏱11am-1am; 🖋; T Chinatown)

Union Park (p95)

Coppa Enoteca

ITALIAN $$

6 ✖ MAP P96, C5

This South End *enoteca* (wine bar) recreates an Italian dining experience with authenticity and innovation, serving up *salumi* (cured meats), antipasti, pasta and other delicious small plates. Wash it all down with an Aperol spritz and you might be tricked into thinking you're in Venice. (☏ 617-391-0902; www.coppaboston.com; 253 Shawmut Ave; small plates $9-17, pizza & pasta $14-25; ⏱ noon-10pm Mon-Thu, to 11pm Fri, 11am-11pm Sat, to 10pm Sun; ☷ SL4, SL5, Ⓣ Back Bay)

Myers + Chang

ASIAN $$

7 ✖ MAP P96, D5

This super-hip Asian spot blends Thai, Chinese and Vietnamese cuisines, which means delicious dumplings, spicy stir-fries and oodles of noodles. The kitchen staff do amazing things with a wok, and the menu of small plates allows you to sample a wide selection of dishes. Dim sum for dinner? This is your place. (☏ 617-542-5200; www.myersandchang.com; 1145 Washington St; small plates $7-17, mains $16-25; ⏱ 5-10pm Sun-Thu, to 11pm Fri & Sat; ⯑ ☷ SL4, SL5, Ⓣ Tufts Medical Center)

Toro

TAPAS $$

8 ✖ MAP P96, B6

True to its Spanish spirit, Toro is bursting with energy, from the open kitchen to the communal butcher-block tables. The menu features simple but sublime tapas – seared foie gras with pistachio and sour cherries; grilled corn on the cob dripping with aioli, lime and cheese; and delectable, garlicky shrimp. Wash it down with rioja, sangria or spiced-up mojitos. (☏ 617-536-4300; www.toro-restaurant.com; 1704 Washington St; tapas $9-16; ⏱ noon-10pm Mon-Thu, to 11pm Fri, 4-11pm Sat, 10:30am-2:30pm & 5-10pm Sun; ⯑ ☷ SL4, SL5, Ⓣ Massachusetts Ave)

Bistro du Midi

FRENCH $$

9 ✖ MAP P96, C1

The upstairs dining room is exquisite, but the downstairs bistro exudes warmth and camaraderie, inviting casual callers to linger over wine and snacks. In either setting, the Provençal fare is artfully presented and delicious. Reservations are required for dinner upstairs, but drop-ins are welcome at the bistro all day. (☏ 617-426-7878; www.bistrodumidi.com; 272 Boylston St; mains bistro $17-34, dining room $29-48; ⏱ bistro 11:30am-10pm, dining room 5-10pm; Ⓣ Arlington)

O Ya

SUSHI $$$

10 ✖ MAP P96, H2

Who knew that raw fish could be so exciting? Here, each piece of nigiri or sashimi is dripped with something unexpected but exquisite, from burgundy truffle sauce to ginger kimchee jus. A fried Kumamoto oyster is topped with a Japanese citrus fruit and squid ink bubbles. Foie gras is drizzled in balsamic chocolate *kabayaki* (sweet, soy glaze). And so on. (📞617-654-9900; www.o-ya. restaurant; 9 East St; nigiri & sashimi pieces $14-30; ⏰5-10pm Tue-Sat; 🚇) 🚇South Station)

Drinking

Beehive COCKTAIL BAR

11 🚇 MAP P96, B5

The Beehive has transformed the basement of the Boston Center for the Arts into a 1920s Paris jazz club. This place is more about the scene than the music, which is often provided by students from Berklee College of Music. But the food is good and the vibe is definitely hip. Reservations required if you want a table. (📞617-423-0069; www.beehiveboston.com; 541 Tremont St; ⏰5pm-midnight Mon-Wed, to 1am Thu, to 2am Fri, 9:30am-2am Sat, to midnight Sun; 🚇Back Bay)

Entertainment

Wally's Café JAZZ

12 ⭐ MAP P96, A4

When Wally's opened in 1947, Barbadian immigrant Joseph Walcott became the first African American to own a nightclub in New England. Old-school, gritty and small, it still attracts a racially diverse crowd to hear jammin' jazz music 365 days a year. Berklee students love this place, especially the nightly jam sessions (6pm to 9pm). (📞617-424-1408; www.wallyscafe.com; 427 Massachusetts Ave; ⏰5pm-2am; 🚇Massachusetts Ave)

Boston Center for the Arts THEATER

13 ⭐ MAP P96, B5

There's rarely a dull moment at the BCA, which serves as a nexus for excellent small theater productions. Over 20 companies present more than 45 separate productions annually, from comedies and drama to modern dance and musicals. The BCA complex comprises several buildings, including a cyclorama (1884) built to display panoramic paintings, a former organ factory and the Mills Gallery (p95). (📞617-426-5000; www.bcaonline.org; 539 Tremont St; 🚇Back Bay)

Charles Playhouse THEATER

14 ⭐ MAP P96, D2

Built in 1839, the Charles Playhouse was originally a speakeasy, later a jazz club and finally a theater. With its backstreet location and underground ambience, it has always been home to offbeat and unusual performances. Nowadays, that means the ever-popular, indefinable **Blue Man**

SoWa Sundays 🛍

Summer Sundays (📞857-362-7692; www.sowaboston.com; 460 Harrison Ave; 🕙10am-4pm Sun May-Oct; 🚍SL4, SL5, 🚇Tufts Medical Center) are lively in the South End. Three different markets fill the art district's parking lots: the **SoWa Open Market** for arts and crafts, **SoWa Farmers Market** for fresh produce and **SoWa Vintage Market** (year-round) for antique treasures. Right nearby, at 530–540 Harrison Ave, you'll find a fabulous Food Truck Bazaar and a summer beer garden.

Group (www.blueman.com) and the long-running improv comedy show **Shear Madness** (www.shearmadness.com). (📞617-426-6912; www.charlesplayhouse.com; 74 Warrenton St; 🚇Boylston)

Wilbur Theatre   COMEDY

15 ✪ MAP P96, E2

The colonial-style Wilbur Theatre dates to 1914, and over the years has hosted many prominent theatrical productions. These days it is Boston's premier comedy club. The smallish house hosts nationally known cutups, as well as music acts and other kinds of hard-to-categorize performances.

The theater itself could do with a renovation, but the talent is good. (📞617-248-9700; www.thewilbur.com; 246 Tremont St; tickets $22-65; 🚇Boylston)

Jacques Cabaret   CABARET

16 ✪ MAP P96, D2

Head to this dive on a dark side street to experience the gay culture of the South End before gentrification took over. A shaded-lamp and pool-table kind of place, Jacques hosts outstanding low-budget drag shows every night. Reservations are a must on weekends. (📞617-426-8902; www.jacques-cabaret.com; 79 Broadway; admission $10-15; 🕙11am-midnight, show times vary; 🚇Arlington)

Shopping

International Poster Gallery   ART

17 🛍 MAP P96, E6

This niche gallery stocks thousands of vintage posters from around the world. Thousands. The posters span the globe, with themes ranging from food and drink to travel to political propaganda. They are all there for the browsing, though it's easier to scroll through the online archive, which also offers all kinds of useful information and tips for would-be collectors. (📞617-375-0076; www.internationalposter.com;

460c Harrison Ave; ⏱10am-6pm Mon-Sat, from noon Sun; 🚌SL4, SL5, Ⓣ Tufts Medical Center)

Sault New England

GIFTS & SOUVENIRS

18 🔒 MAP P96, B5

Blending prepster and hipster, rustic and chic, this little basement boutique packs in a lot of intriguing stuff. The eclectic mix of merchandise runs the gamut from new and vintage clothing to coffee-table books and homemade terrariums. A New England theme runs through the store, with nods to the Kennedys, *Jaws* and LL Bean. (📞857-239-9434; www.saultne.com; 577 Tremont St; ⏱10am-7pm Mon-Sat, to 5pm Sun; Ⓣ Back Bay)

Olives & Grace

GIFTS & SOUVENIRS

19 🔒 MAP P96, A6

This little shoebox of a store offers an eclectic array of gift items – many from New England – all of them made with love and thoughtfulness by artisans. The most enticing items are the foodstuffs, including chocolate bars, hot sauces, raw honey, saltwater taffy and cocktail mixers. All the good stuff. (📞617-236-4536; www.olivesandgrace.com; 623 Tremont St; ⏱10am-8pm Tue-Sat, to 6pm Sun & Mon; Ⓣ Back Bay)

SoWa Farmers Market

STEPHAN SCHLACHTER/SHUTTERSTOCK ©

Explore ◎
Back Bay

Back Bay includes the city's most fashionable window-shopping, latte-drinking and people-watching area, on Newbury St, as well as its most elegant architecture, around Copley Square. Its streets lined with stately brownstones and shaded by magnolia trees, it is among Boston's most prestigious addresses. For fresh air and riverside strolling, head to the Charles River Esplanade.

Short List

○ **Copley Square (p112)** Admiring Boston's most evocative and archetypal architecture in this centerpiece square.

○ **Charles River Esplanade (p112)** Strolling, cycling or running along the waterfront.

○ **Saltie Girl (p115)** Squeezing into a seat at this fantastic 'seafood bar' to sample the city's most inventive local fare.

○ **Mapparium (p112)** Feeling like you're at the center of the world at this odd but intriguing piece of history.

○ **Courtyard (p115)** Indulging in afternoon tea within the exquisite walls of the Boston Public Library.

Getting There & Around

Ⓜ The main branch of the green line runs the length of Boylston St, with stops at Arlington near the Public Garden, Copley at Copley Square and Hynes at Mass Ave. The orange line is also useful for the Back Bay/South End stop in the southern part of the neighborhood.

Neighborhood Map on p110

Copley Square (p112) JON BILOUS/SHUTTERSTOCK ©

Top Experience 📷
Wander the Stacks at Boston Public Library

The esteemed Boston Public Library (BPL) was founded in 1852 as a 'shrine of letters.' The old McKim Building is notable for its magnificent fa-cade (inspired by Italian Renaissance palazzi) and exquisite interior art. Pick up a free brochure and take a self-guided tour; alternatively, free guided tours depart from the entrance hall (times vary).

◉ MAP P110, E4

☎ 617-536-5400

www.bpl.org

700 Boylston St

admission free

🕐 9am-9pm Mon-Thu, to 5pm Fri & Sat year-round, plus 1-5pm Sun Oct-May

🇹 Copley

Puis de Chavannes Gallery

From the main entrance, a marble staircase leads past Pierre Puvis de Chavannes' inspirational mural depicting poetry, philosophy, history and science. Upstairs, at the entrance to Bates Hall, there is another Puvis de Chavannes mural; here, the nine muses from Greek mythology are honoring a male figure, the Genius of the Enlightenment.

Bates Hall

The staircase terminates at the splendid Bates Hall Reading Room (pictured), where even mundane musings are elevated by the barrel-vaulted, 50ft coffered ceilings. Joshua Bates was the BPL's original benefactor, stipulating that 'the building shall be...an ornament to the city, that there shall be a room for 100 to 150 persons to sit at reading tables, and that it shall be perfectly free to all.'

Abbey Room

The Abbey Room is among the library's most sumptuous, with its oak wainscoting, checkerboard marble floors, elaborate fireplace and coffered ceiling inspired by the Doge's Palace in Venice. The room is named for the artist responsible for the 1895 murals, which recount Sir Galahad's *Quest and Achievement of the Holy Grail*.

Sargent Gallery

The pièce de résistance of the BPL art collection is on the 3rd floor, which features John Singer Sargent's unfinished Judaic and Christian murals entitled *The Triumph of Religion*. The murals trace the history of Western religion, from paganism to Judaism to Christiantiy. A final painting was intended for the vacant space above the stairwell, but it was never completed, due in part to criticism from the Jewish community.

★ Top Tips

○ The BPL offers free guided art and architecture tours, leaving from the entrance hall at various times throughout the week; see the BPL website for a current schedule.

○ The special collections hold countless treasures, including John Adams' personal library. Also look out for free events, from author talks to musical performances.

○ Don't leave without taking a moment of contemplation in the peaceful Italianate courtyard.

✕ Take a Break

Grab a coffee, sandwich or salad at the on-site **Map Room Cafe** (www.thecateredaffair.com/bpl; snacks, salads & sandwiches $6-12; ◷9am-5pm Mon-Sat; 🛜🍴).

For an exquisite afternoon tea, head to the more formal Courtyard (p115).

Top Experience 📷
Marvel at the Murals in Trinity Church

The country's ultimate example of Richardsonian Romanesque, Trinity Church is acclaimed for its integrated composition of shapes, colors and textures, the result of a cooperative effort by artist John LaFarge and architect Henry Hobson Richardson. The granite exterior employs sandstone in colorful patterns, while the interior presents an awe-inspiring array of vibrant murals and stained glass.

◎ MAP P110, F4

www.trinitychurch
boston.org

206 Clarendon St

adult/child $10/free

🕙10am-4:30pm Tue-Sat,
12:15-4:30pm Sun Easter-
Oct, reduced hours rest
of year

Architecture

The footprint of Trinity Church is a Greek cross, with chancel, nave and transepts surrounding the central square. The wide-open interior was a radical departure from traditional Episcopal architecture, but it embodies the democratic spirit of the congregation in the 1870s.

LaFarge Murals

The walls of the great central tower are covered by two tiers of murals, soaring more than 100ft high. Prior to this commission, LaFarge did not have experience with mural painting on this scale. The result – thousands of square feet of exquisite, jewel-toned encaustic paintings – established his authority as the father of the American mural movement.

Stained-Glass Windows

The 33 stained-glass windows – mostly executed by different glass workshops – represent diverse styles. The original windows from 1877 and 1878 are the traditional European designs, completed by premier English workshops. Several later examples represent the English arts-and-crafts movement, while the ornate French windows were designed by Parisian artist Achille François Oudinot.

The jewels of the church are the work of LaFarge, distinctive for their use of layered opalescent glass, resulting in an unprecedented richness of shades and dimensions. LaFarge's first commission was *Christ in Majesty*, the spectacular three-panel clerestory window at the western end that is now considered one of the USA's finest examples of stained-glass art.

★ **Top Tips**

o Free architectural tours are offered on Sunday at 12:30pm. Additional tours are offered daily throughout the week (times vary).

o Free concerts on the impressive pipe organ are held on Fridays at 12:15pm, with additional ticketed concerts throughout the year.

o Snap a photo from Clarendon St to catch the exquisite church reflected in the facade of the nearby **John Hancock Tower** (200 Clarendon St).

✕ **Take a Break**

Stop for sustenance at Flour (p114), which gets rave reviews for rich coffee, fresh-made scones and pastries, and delectable, satisfying soups and sandwiches.

For a more substantial meal, head down Boylston St to Atlantic Fish Co (p115), where you can feast on crab cakes, chowder and lobster ravioli.

For reviews see
◉ Top Experiences	p106
◎ Sights	p112
✕ Eating	p113
☕ Drinking	p116
☆ Entertainment	p118
🛍 Shopping	p118

Charles River

Charles River Bike Path

Beacon St

Storrow Dr

Back St

Marlborough St

BACK BAY

Beacon St

Marlborough St

Hereford St

Gloucester St

Fairfield St

Commonwealth Ave

Commonwealth Ave Mall

Commonwealth Ave

Exeter St

24

22

11 ✕ ✕ 6

19

Newbury St

✕ 9

13 ✕

Boylston St

Ring Rd

5

20

23

17

Hynes Convention Center

Massachusetts Turnpike

Hynes Convention Center

Boston Duck Tours

18

16

Dalton St

Scotia St

Prudential Center Skywalk Observatory

3

Sheraton Boston Hotel

Haviland St

Belvidere St

St Germain St

Huntington Ave

Prudential

Norway St

Edgerly Rd

Clearway St

4

Mary Baker Eddy Library & Mapparium

Public Alley 402

W Newton St

St Botolph St

Burbank St

Massachusetts Ave

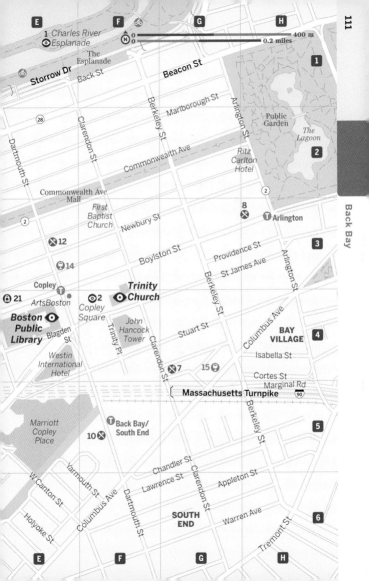

Back Bay

E
F
G
H

1 Charles River
Esplanade

N 0   400 m
  0   0.2 miles

The Esplanade

Storrow Dr

Beacon St

Back St

Marlborough St

Berkeley St

Arlington St

Public Garden

The Lagoon

Clarendon St

Commonwealth Ave

Ritz Carlton Hotel

Dartmouth St

Commonwealth Ave Mall

First Baptist Church

Newbury St

8

Arlington

12

Boylston St

Providence St

St James Ave

Arlington St

14

Copley

ArtsBoston

21

Trinity Church

2

Copley Square

Stuart St

Berkeley St

Columbus Ave

BAY VILLAGE

Boston Public Library

John Hancock Tower

Blagden St

Trinity Pl

Clarendon St

Isabella St

Westin International Hotel

7

15

Cortes St

Marginal Rd

Massachusetts Turnpike

90

Marriott Copley Place

Back Bay/ South End

10

W Canton St

Yarmouth St

Columbus Ave

Chandler St

Lawrence St

Clarendon St

Appleton St

Berkeley St

Dartmouth St

SOUTH END

Warren Ave

Tremont St

Holyoke St

E
F
G
H

Sights

Charles River Esplanade

PARK

1 ⊚ MAP P110, E1

The southern bank of the Charles River Basin is an enticing urban escape, with grassy knolls and cooling waterways, all designed by Frederick Law Olmsted. It stretches almost 3 miles along the Boston shore of the Charles River, from the Museum of Science to Boston University Bridge. The park is dotted with public art, including an oversized bust of Arthur Fiedler, longtime conductor of the Boston Pops. Paths along the river are ideal for bicycling, jogging or walking. The **Hatch Memorial Shell** often has free shows in summer. (www.esplanadeassociation.org; ⛹; T Charles/MGH, Kenmore)

Copley Square

PLAZA

2 ⊚ MAP P110, F4

Here you'll find a cluster of handsome historic buildings, including the ornate French-Romanesque Trinity Church (p108), the masterwork of architect HH Richardson. Across the street, the classic Boston Public Library (p106) was America's first municipal library. Pick up a self-guided tour brochure and wander around, noting gems like the murals by John Singer Sargent and sculpture by Augustus Saint-Gaudens. (T Copley)

Prudential Center Skywalk Observatory

VIEWPOINT

3 ⊚ MAP P110, C5

Technically called the Shops at Prudential Center, this landmark Boston building is not much more than a fancy shopping mall. But it does provide a bird's-eye view of Boston from its 50th-floor Skywalk. Completely enclosed by glass, the Skywalk offers spectacular 360-degree views of Boston and Cambridge, accompanied by an entertaining audiotour (with a special version catering to kids). Alternatively, you can enjoy the same view from Top of the Hub (p117) for the price of a drink. (www.skywalkboston.com; 800 Boylston St; adult/child $20/14; ⊙10am-10pm Mar-Oct, to 8pm Nov-Feb; P ⛹; T Prudential)

Mary Baker Eddy Library & Mapparium

LIBRARY

4 ⊚ MAP P110, B6

The Mary Baker Eddy Library houses one of Boston's hidden treasures. The intriguing Mapparium is a room-sized, stained-glass globe that visitors walk through on a glass bridge. It was created in 1935, which is reflected in the globe's geopolitical boundaries. The acoustics, which surprised even the designer, allow everyone in the room to hear even the tiniest whisper. (☎617-450-7000; www.marybakereddylibrary.org; 200 Massachusetts Ave; adult/child $6/4; ⊙10am-5pm; ⛹; T Symphony)

Eating

Luke's Lobster

SEAFOOD $

5 ⊗ MAP P110, D4

Luke Holden took a Maine seafood shack and put it in the middle of Back Bay (and other places around Boston), so that hungry shoppers could get a classic lobster roll for lunch. The place looks authentic, with weathered wood interior and nautical decor, but more importantly, the lobster rolls are the real deal – and afford-able. The only thing lacking is sea breezes. (☎857-350-4626; www.lukeslobster.com; 75 Exeter St; mains $9-19; ◷11am-9pm Sun-Wed, to 10pm Thu-Sat; Ⓣ Copley)

Dirty Water Dough Co

PIZZA $

6 ⊗ MAP P110, D4

If there's anything that Bostonians love more than the Standells, it's pizza. That explains why the kids are lining up to get theirs from Dirty Water Dough, where they can get a big slice and a soda for $5. Other perks: locally sourced ingredients, unusual topping combos and gluten-free options, not to mention the Dirty Water IPA. (☎617-262-0090; www.dirtywaterdough.com; 222 Newbury St; slices $3-4, pizzas $11-15; ◷11am-10pm Sun-Thu, to 11pm Fri & Sat; ♫; Ⓣ Copley)

Charles River Esplanade

Weather or Not

Steady blue, clear view/ Flashing blue, clouds are due/ Steady red, rain ahead/Flashing red, snow instead.

Part of the local lore since 1950, Bostonians have used this simple rhyme and the weather beacon atop the Old Hancock Building – next to the John Hancock Tower – to determine if they need to take their umbrella when they leave the house. And yes, the beacon has been known to flash red in midsummer, but that is not a warning of some extremely inclement New England weather, but rather an indication that the Red Sox game has been canceled for the night.

Flour

BAKERY $

7 ❌ MAP P110, G4

Joanne Chang's beloved bakery is taking over Boston. This outlet – on the edge of Back Bay – has the same flaky pastries and rich coffee that we have come to expect, not to mention sandwiches, soups, salads and pizzas. And just to prove there is something for everybody, Flour also sells housemade dog biscuits for your canine friend. (☏617-437-7700; www.flourbakery. com; 131 Clarendon St; pastries from $3.50, sandwiches $9.50; ⏱6:30am-8pm Mon-Fri, 8am-6pm Sat, to 5pm Sun; 🛜🚭♿; Ⓣ Back Bay)

Parish Café

SANDWICHES $

8 ❌ MAP P110, H3

Sample the creations of Boston's most famous chefs without exhausting your expense account. The menu at Parish features a rotating roster of salads and sandwiches, each designed by local celebrity chefs, including Jamie Bissonnette, Barbara Lynch and Tony Maws. The place feels more 'pub' than 'cafe,' with a long bar backed by big TVs and mirrors. (☏617-247-4777; www.parishcafe.com; 361 Boylston St; sandwiches $12-20; ⏱11:30am-1am, bar to 2am; 🚭; Ⓣ Arlington)

Puro Ceviche Bar

LATIN AMERICAN $$

9 ❌ MAP P110, C4

This bar serves up delightfully modern yet still authentic Latin American fare in its funky downstairs digs, where exposed brick walls are covered with bold murals. Choose between six types of *ceviche*, six kinds of tacos and a slew of Latin-inspired small plates. Also on offer are classic cocktails and a nicely curated wine list. Attention, budget-minded travelers: $2 tacos on Tuesdays. (☏617-266-0707; www. purocevichebar.com; 264 Newbury St; small plates $10-16; ⏱4-11pm Mon-Thu, 11am-11pm Fri-Sun; Ⓣ Hynes)

Salty Pig

ITALIAN $$

10 ❌ MAP P110, F5

With prosciutto, pâté, *rillettes*, *testa* (head cheese), *sanguinaccio* (blood sausage), *porchetta* (pork shoulder) and more, you'll feel like you're in one of those cultures that eats every part of the animal. 'Salty Pig Parts' get paired with stinky cheeses and other accompaniments for amazing charcuterie plates. There's pizza and pasta for the less adventurous, and cocktails and craft beers too. (☏617-536-6200; www.thesaltypig.com; 130 Dartmouth St; charcuterie $7, mains $12-19; ☉11:30am-midnight; Ⓣ Back Bay)

Piattini   ITALIAN $$

11 ❌ MAP P110, D4

If you have trouble deciding what to order, Piattini can help. The name means 'small plates,' so you don't have to choose just one. There's also an enticing array of pasta dishes, as well as an extensive list of wines by the glass. This intimate *enoteca* (wine bar) and its patio are delightful settings to sample the flavors of Italy. (☏617-536-2020; www.piattini.com; 226 Newbury St; small plates $9-16, pasta $20-28; ☉11am-10pm; ☕; Ⓣ Copley)

Saltie Girl   SEAFOOD $$$

12 ❌ MAP P110, E3

Here's a new concept in dining: the seafood bar. It's a delightfully intimate place to feast on tantalizing dishes that blow away all preconceived notions about seafood. From your traditional Gloucester lobster roll to tinned fish on toast

to the irresistible torched salmon belly, this place is full of delightful surprises.

Reservations are not accepted and the place is tiny, so expect to wait. (It's worth it.) (☏617-267-0691; www.saltiegirl.com; 281 Dartmouth St; small plates $12-18, mains $18-40; ☉11:30am-10pm; Ⓣ Copley)

Courtyard   AMERICAN $$$

The perfect destination for an elegant afternoon tea is – believe it or not – the Boston Public Library (see ☉ Map p110, E4). Overlooking the beautiful Italianate courtyard, this grown-up restaurant serves an artfully prepared selection of sandwiches, scones and sweets, accompanied by a wide range of teas (black, green and herbal). Reserve ahead, especially on weekends. (☏617-859-2251; www.thecateredaffair.com/bpl; 700 Boylston St; tea adult/child $39/19; ☉11:30am-5pm Mon-Sat, 1-5pm Sun; Ⓣ Copley)

Atlantic Fish Co   SEAFOOD $$$

13 ❌ MAP P110, D4

New England clam chowder in a bread bowl: for a perfect lunch here, that's all you need to know. For nonbelievers, we'll add seafood *fra diavolo*, lobster ravioli and local Jonah crab cakes. There's more, of course, and the menu is printed daily to showcase the freshest ingredients. Enjoy eating in the dining room or on the flower-filled sidewalk patio.

Boston Marathon ⓘ

One of the country's most prestigious marathons takes runners on a 26.2-mile course ending at Copley Sq on Patriots' Day, a Massachusetts holiday on the third Monday in April.

The race starts in rural Hopkinton, MA, and winds its way through the western suburbs to Boston. Some of the marathon's most dramatic moments occur between mile 20 and 21, when the aptly named Heartbreak Hill rises a steep 80ft. It's all downhill from there. Runners cruise up Beacon St, through Kenmore Sq, down 'Comm Ave' (Commonwealth Ave), over to Boylston St, and into a triumphant finish at Copley Sq. This final mile is among the most exciting places to watch.

In 2013 the nation (and the world) turned their eyes to Boston when two bombs exploded near the finish line of the Boston Marathon, killing three and injuring hundreds. Several days later, a Massachusetts Institute of Technology (MIT) police officer was shot dead and the entire city was locked down as Boston became a battleground for the 'War on Terror'. The tragedy was devastating, but Boston claimed countless heroes, especially the many victims who inspired others with their courage throughout their recoveries.

(☎617-267-4000; www.atlanticfish.com; 761 Boylston St; mains lunch $16-28, dinner $22-44; ☺11:30am-11pm; Ⓣ Copley)

Drinking

Lolita Cocina & Tequila Bar
COCKTAIL BAR

14 Ⓜ MAP P110, E3

This spicy little Mexican number is full of surprises (which we won't ruin for you). We will reveal that there are no less than ten different margaritas on offer, including the eye-popping Diablo. The menu is packed with unusual and enticing Mexican fare that does not disappoint. Oh, and there's all-you-can-eat tacos for $9 on (most) Monday nights. (www.lolitamexican.com; 271 Dartmouth St; ☺4pm-midnight, bar to 2am; Ⓣ Copley)

Club Café
GAY

15 Ⓜ MAP P110, G4

It's a club! It's a cafe! It's a cabaret! Anything goes at this glossy, gay nightlife extravaganza. There is live cabaret in the Napoleon Room six nights a week, while the main dance and lounge area has tea parties, salsa dancing, trivia competitions, karaoke, drag bingo and good old-fashioned dance parties. (📞617-536-0966; www.clubcafe.com; 209 Columbus Ave; ⏰11am-2am; 🇹Back Bay)

Bukowski Tavern

BAR

16 🚇 MAP P110, B5

This sweet bar lies inside a parking garage next to the canyon of the Mass Pike. Expect sticky wooden tables, loud rock music, black hoodies, cussing, a dozen different burgers and dogs, and more than 100 kinds of beer. In God we trust, all others pay cash.

(📞617-437-9999; www.bukowskitavern.net; 50 Dalton St; ⏰11:30am-2am Mon-Sat, from noon Sun; 🇹Hynes)

Top of the Hub

BAR

Yes, it's touristy. And overpriced. And the food is not too inspiring. But the head-spinning city view makes it worthwhile to ride the elevator up to the 52nd floor of the Prudential Center (see 3 ⊙ Map p110, C5). Come for spectacular sunset drinks and stay for free live jazz. Beware the $24 per-person minimum after 8pm. (📞617-536-1775; www.topofthehub.net; 800 Boylston St; ⏰11:30am-1am; 📶; 🇹Prudential)

Boston Marathon

Entertainment

Red Room @ Cafe 939

LIVE MUSIC

17 😊 MAP P110, B4

Run by Berklee students, the Red Room @ Cafe 939 has emerged as one of Boston's least predictable and most enjoyable music venues. It has an excellent sound system and a baby grand piano; most importantly, it books interesting, eclectic up-and-coming musicians. Buy tickets in advance at the Berklee Performance Center. (📞617-747-2261; www.berklee.edu/cafe939; 939 Boylston St; tickets free-$20; 🕑box office 10am-6pm Mon-Sat; Ⓣ Hynes)

Berklee Performance Center

CONCERT VENUE

18 😊 MAP P110, B5

The performance hall at this notable music college hosts a wide variety of performances, from high-energy jazz recitals and songs by smoky-throated vocalists to oddball sets by keyboard-tapping guys who look like their day job is dungeon master. (📞617-747-2261; www.berklee.edu/bpc; 136 Massachusetts Ave; tickets $10-65; 🕑box office 10am-6pm Mon-Sat; Ⓣ Hynes)

Shopping

Topdrawer

GIFTS & SOUVENIRS

19 🔒 MAP P110, C4

Travelers! Here is a store full of things you need, even if you didn't realize you needed them. Everything from plush fold-up slippers (perfect for chilly airplanes) to fabulous, functional daypacks and travel pouches. The aesthetic is modern and minimalist, but you'll also find an appealingly old-fashioned selection of pen sets and travel journals to record all your memories. (📞857-305-3934; www.kolo.com; 273 Newbury St; 🕑11am-7pm; Ⓣ Hynes)

Trident Booksellers & Café

BOOKS

20 🔒 MAP P110, A4

Pick out a pile of books and retreat to a quiet corner of the cafe to decide which ones you really want to buy. There's a little bit of everything here, and the 'hippie turned back-to-the-lander, turned Buddhist, turned entrepreneur' owners really know how to keep their customers happy. (📞617-267-8688; www.tridentbookscafe.com; 338 Newbury St; 🕑8am-midnight; 📶; Ⓣ Hynes)

Discount Tickets

Visit **ArtsBoston** (Map p110, E4; www.artsboston.org; 650 Boylston St; 🕑11am-5pm Thu & Fri, 10am-4pm Sat & Sun; Ⓣ Copley) on Copley Square or at Quincy Market for same-day, discounted tickets to local theater, comedy and music events.

Marathon Sports

SPORTS & OUTDOORS

21 🔒 MAP P110, E4

Specializing in running gear, this place could not have a better location: it overlooks the finish line of the Boston Marathon. It's known for attentive customer service, as staff work hard to make sure you get a shoe that fits. They also work hard to support the running community, with a weekly running club and a calendar of other events. (📞617-267-4774; www.marathonsports.com; 671 Boylston St; ⏰10am-7:30pm Mon-Wed & Fri, to 8pm Thu & Sat, 11am-6pm Sun; Ⓣ Copley)

KitchenWares

HOMEWARES

22 🔒 MAP P110, D3

KitchenWares is popular for its selection of cutlery, as well as its all-important knife sharpening service. Less known, it's also an excellent spot for unusual gifts and souvenirs, such as lobster-shaped cookie cutters, Fenway Park coasters and beautiful, copper Boston-style cocktail shakers. (📞857-366-4237; www.kitchen-waresboston.com; 215 Newbury St; ⏰10am-7pm Mon-Sat, noon-5pm Sun; Ⓣ Copley)

Newbury Comics

MUSIC

23 🔒 MAP P110, B4

How does a music store remain relevant in the digital world? One word: vinyl. In addition to the many cheap CDs and DVDs, there's a solid selection of new-release vinyl. Incidentally, it does sell comic books, as well as T-shirts, action figures and silly gags. No wonder everyone is having such a wicked good time. (📞617-236-4930; www.newburycomics.com; 332 Newbury St; ⏰10am-10pm Mon-Sat, 11am-8pm Sun; Ⓣ Hynes)

Hempest

CONCEPT STORE

24 🔒 MAP P110, D3

The Hempest is not a well-stocked smoke shop, though there is a small selection of pipes and bongs. It's more about stylish clothing, organic soaps and lotions, and fun home-furnishing items. Most of the products are made from cannabis hemp, the botanical cousin of marijuana. (📞617-421-9944; www.hempest.com; 207 Newbury St; ⏰11am-7pm Mon-Sat, noon-6pm Sun; Ⓣ Copley)

Explore ◉

Kenmore Square & Fenway

Kenmore Sq and Fenway attract club-goers and baseball fans to the streets surrounding Fenway Park. At the other end of the neighborhood, art lovers and culture-vultures flock to the artistic institutions along the Avenue of the Arts (Huntington Ave), including the Museum of Fine Arts and Symphony Hall.

Short List

○ *Museum of Fine Arts (p122)* Exploring the Art of the Americas and discovering other treasures.

○ *Fenway Park (p126)* Watching the Red Sox whip their opponents at America's oldest ballpark.

○ *Isabella Stewart Gardner Museum (p124)* Venerating Gardner's artistic, aesthetic and cultural legacy.

○ *Boston Symphony Orchestra (p131)* Hearing the world-renowned orchestra play at Symphony Hall.

○ *Lansdowne St (p130)* Heading out for a night of drinking at Cheeky Monkey or music at House of Blues.

Getting There & Around

Ⓜ To reach Kenmore Sq or Fenway Park, take any of the green line trains except the E branch to Kenmore T station. Sights along Huntington Ave in Fenway are accessible from the E-branch Museum of Fine Arts stop or the orange-line Ruggles station.

Neighborhood Map on p128

Symphony Hall, home of the Boston Symphony Orchestra (p131)
JOSEPH SOHM/SHUTTERSTOCK ©

Top Experience 📷
Unleash Your Culture Vulture at the MFA

Since 1876, the Museum of Fine Arts (MFA) has been Boston's premier venue for showcasing art by local, national and international artists. Nowadays, the museum's holdings encompass all eras, making it truly encyclopedic in scope. Gorgeous modern wings dedicated to the Art of the Americas and to contemporary art have contributed to Boston's emergence as an art center in the 21st century.

◎ MAP P128, C4

☏ 617-267-9300

www.mfa.org

465 Huntington Ave

adult/child $25/free

🕐 10am-5pm Sat-Tue, to 10pm Wed-Fri

T Museum of Fine Arts; Ruggles

Art of the Americas

The centerpiece of the MFA. On the second level is an entire gallery is dedicated to John Singer Sargent. Highlights in the American Impressionism galleries include pieces by Mary Cassat and the perennial local favorite, *At Dusk* by Childe Hassam. The top floor is devoted to modernism, including impressive additions by Latin American artists.

Art of Europe

The Italian Renaissance is well represented, as is the Dutch Golden Age, with five paintings by Rembrandt. The highlights of the European exhibit are the Impressionists and Postimpressionists, with masterpieces by Degas, Gauguin, Renoir and van Gogh, and a sizable collection of Monets (one of the largest outside Paris).

Art of Asia, Oceania & Africa

The centerpiece is the peaceful Buddhist Temple room on the 2nd floor, just one exhibit in a vast array of Japanese art, including prints and metalworks. There is also an extensive display of Chinese paintings, calligraphy and ceramics.

Art of the Ancient World

The highlight is certainly the Egyptian galleries, especially the two rooms of mummies. In the first half of the 20th century, the MFA and Harvard University cooperated to excavate tombs and temples surrounding the Giza Pyramids, bringing back thousands of artifacts that are now on display.

Linde Family Wing for Contemporary Art

The 2011 renovation of the MFA's west wing nearly tripled the exhibition space for contemporary art. The darling of museum patrons is *Black River,* a fantastic woven tapestry of discarded bottle caps, by Ghanaian artist El Anatsui.

★ Top Tips

o You can rent a guided multimedia tour (adult/child $6/4) in one of 10 languages. Live guided tours are also available throughout the day.

o Children under the age of 17 are admitted free after 3pm on weekdays and all day on weekends.

o Before jumping into the collections, stop to admire the murals in the rotunda and above the main staircase, all painted by John Singer Sargent.

✗ Take a Break

The Linde Wing features upscale dining at the restaurant **Bravo** (mains $21-31; ⏱11:30am-3pm daily, 5:30-8:30pm Wed-Fri) as well as a cafeteria.

In the spacious, glass-enclosed Shapiro Family Courtyard, sample modern American cuisine at the **New American Café** (sandwiches $16-18, mains $17-26; ⏱11:30am-4pm Sat-Tue, to 8pm Wed-Fri).

Top Experience 📷
Admire the Art at Isabella Stewart Gardner Museum

The magnificent Venetian-style palazzo that houses this museum was home to Isabella Stewart Gardner herself until her death in 1924. A monument to one woman's taste for acquiring exquisite art, the Gardner is filled with some 2500 priceless objects, primarily European. The four-story greenhouse courtyard is a tranquil oasis.

◉ MAP P128, B4

📞 617-566-1401

www.gardnermuseum.org

25 Evans Way

adult/child $15/free

🕐 11am-5pm Wed-Mon, to 9pm Thu

Ⓣ Museum of Fine Arts

Cloister

On the 1st floor, the Spanish Cloister is paved with striking Islamic tiles. At one end, a Moorish arch frames John Singer Sargent's painting *El Jaleo*. At the other end, a wrought-iron gate leads into the Spanish Chapel, hung with Spanish religious art.

2nd Floor

On the 2nd floor, the **Dutch room** contains Isabella's small collection of Dutch and Flemish art, including a self-portrait by Rembrandt and another portrait by Rubens. Note the empty frames, where stolen paintings once hung. The majestic **Tapestry Room** evokes a castle hall, hung with 10 allegorical tapestries.

3rd Floor

The 3rd floor contains the highlights of this rich collection. The sumptuous **Veronese Room** is so named for the stunning ceiling painting, but this room is filled with treasures, including pastels by James McNeill Whistler.

The museum's most celebrated gallery is the **Titian Room**, centered on Titian's famous rendition of *Europa*. Your final stop is the **Gothic Room**, featuring Sargent's remarkable portrait of Isabella herself.

Museum Heist

On March 18, 1990, two thieves disguised as police officers broke into the Isabella Stewart Gardner Museum. They left with nearly $200 million worth of artworks. The most famous painting stolen was Vermeer's *The Concert*, but the loot also included three works by Rembrandt, and others by Manet and Degas, not to mention French and Chinese artifacts. The crime was never solved. Since Isabella's will stipulated that the exhibit should never be altered, the empty frames still hang on the walls.

★ Top Tips

○ Admission to the Gardner is free on your birthday! If your name is Isabella, admission is free every day.

○ Free tours and public talks are offered nearly every day, including the 45-minute 'Collection Conversations' on weekdays at 2pm.

○ Decked with ancient art and seasonal blooms, the courtyard (pictured) is glorious from any angle. Check it out from the upper-story windows.

✗ Take a Break

If there isn't a free table at the elegant **Café G** (mains $16-18; ⊙11am-4pm Wed-Mon, to 8pm Thu) on the museum's ground floor, you'll be given a pager so you can explore the palazzo until your table is ready.

Alternatively, exit the museum and stroll across the Back Bay Fens for a quick but satisfying lunch at El Pelon (p129).

Top Experience 📷
Soak Up the Atmosphere at Fenway Park

What is it that makes Fenway Park 'America's Most Beloved Ballpark'? It's not just that it's the home of the Boston Red Sox. Open since 1912, it's the oldest operating baseball park in the country. To learn more, take the hour-long tour of this beloved Boston landmark. Bonus: see the ballpark from atop the legendary Green Monster!

◉ MAP P128, C1

www.redsox.com

4 Jersey St

tours adult/child $20/14, pre-game $35-45

🕘 9am-5pm Apr-Oct, special schedule game days, 10am-5pm Nov-Mar

🇹 Kenmore

Green Monster

As all Red Sox fans know, 'the wall giveth and the wall taketh away.' The 37ft-high left-field wall is only 310ft away from home plate (compared to the standard 325ft), so it's popular among right-handed hitters, who can score an easy home run with a high hit to left. However, batters can just as easily be deprived of a home run when a powerful but low line drive bounces off the Monster for an off-the-wall double.

The Green Monster was painted green in 1947 and since then it has become a patented part of the Fenway experience. Literally. The color is officially known as 'Fence Green' and the supplier will not share the formula.

At the base of the Green Monster is the original scoreboard, still updated manually from behind the wall.

The Triangle

Many a double has turned into a triple when the ball has flown into the deepest, darkest corner of center field (where the walls form a triangle). At 425ft, it's the furthest distance from home plate.

Pesky Pole

The Pesky Pole, Fenway's right-field foul pole, is named for former shortstop Johnny Pesky. Johnny 'Mr Red Sox' Pesky was associated with the team for 15 years as a player and 46 as a manager, coach and special instructor, until his death in 2012.

Lone Red Seat

The bleachers at Fenway Park are green, except for one lone red seat: seat 21 at section 42, row 37. This is supposedly the longest home run ever hit at Fenway Park – officially 502ft, hit by Red Sox left fielder Ted Williams in 1946.

★ Top Tips

○ Tours depart at the top of the hour. Buy tickets online or at the Gate D ticket booth.

○ If you want to see a game, it's best to buy tickets well in advance. Game-day tickets go on sale (one per person) at Gate E, 90 minutes before the game, but people start lining up five hours ahead of time.

○ On game days, you can watch the teams warm up if you join a special 'pre-game tour' ($35).

✕ Take a Break

Concessions line the ballpark's breezeway, selling hot dogs, nachos, pretzels and beer.

Outside the ballpark, you'll find food and drink at the Bleacher Bar (p130) or any of the joints along Lansdowne St.

Kenmore Square & Fenway Soak Up the Atmosphere at Fenway Park

Kenmore Square & Fenway

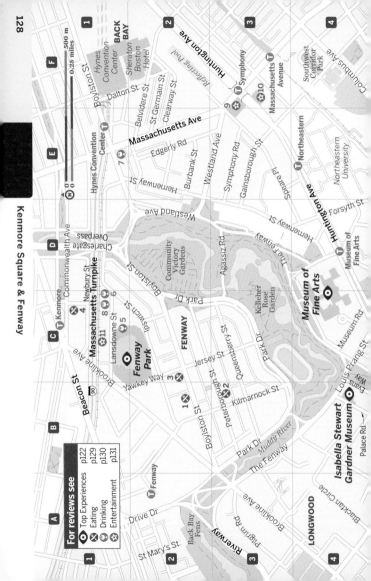

0 0.25 miles
0 500 m

BACK BAY

Hynes Convention Center
Sheraton Boston Hotel
Boylston St
Dalton St
Belvidere St
St Germain St
Clearway St

Reflecting Pool
Huntington Ave

Symphony
10
9
Massachusetts Avenue
Southwest Corridor Park
Columbus Ave

Hynes Convention Center
Massachusetts Ave
7
Edgerly Rd
Burbank St
Westland Ave
Symphony Rd
Gainsborough St
Hemenway St
Symphony Pl
Speare Pl

Northeastern
Northeastern University
Huntington Ave
Forsyth St

Commonwealth Ave
Charlesgate Overpass
Westland Ave

Community Victory Gardens
Agassiz Rd
The Fenway
Hemenway St

Museum of Fine Arts
Museum of Fine Arts

Kenmore
Newbury St
Massachusetts Turnpike
4
6
8
Boylston St
Park Dr
Kelleher Rose Garden

Brookline Ave
Beacon St
90
Lansdowne St
11
Ipswich St
5

Fenway Park
Yawkey Way
FENWAY
Jersey St
Queensberry St
Park Dr
Museum Rd
Louis Prang St
Evans Way
Palace Rd

3
1
2
Kilmarnock St
Peterborough St

Isabella Stewart Gardner Museum

Fenway
Boylston St
Park Dr
Muddy River
The Fenway
Blackan Circle

LONGWOOD

Drive Dr
Back Bay Fens
Riverway
Brookline Ave
Pilgrim Rd

St Mary's St

Eating

Eventide Fenway

SEAFOOD **$**

1 ⊗ MAP P128, B2

James Beard award winners Mike Wiley and Andrew Taylor opened this counter-service version of their beloved Maine seafood restaurant. Fast, fresh and fabulous, the menu features just-shucked oysters and brown-butter lobster rolls, along with some pretty sophisticated seafood specials. Wash it down with a craft beer or a glass of rosé and the whole experience feels (and tastes) gourmet. (📞617-545-1060; www.eventideoysterco.com; 1321 Boylston St; mains $9-16; ⏱11am-11pm; 🛜; 🇹Fenway)

El Pelon

MEXICAN **$**

2 ⊗ MAP P128, B3

If your budget is tight, don't miss this chance to fill up on Boston's best burritos, tacos and tortas, made with the freshest ingredients. The *tacos de la casa* are highly recommended, especially the *pescado,* made with crispy cod and topped with chili mayo. Plates are paper and cutlery is plastic. (📞617-262-9090; www.elpelon.com; 92 Peterborough St; mains $6-9; ⏱11am-11pm; 🍴; 🇹Fenway)

Tasty Burger

BURGERS **$**

3 ⊗ MAP P128, C2

Once a Mobil gas station, this place is now a retro burger joint, with picnic tables outside and a pool table inside. The name is

Oysters with lemon

VIVVI SMAK/SHUTTERSTOCK ©

a nod to *Pulp Fiction*, as is the wall-mounted poster of Samuel L Jackson, whose character would surely agree that 'this is a tasty burger.' (📞617-425-4444; www.tastyburger.com; 1301 Boylston St; burgers $5-6; 🕐11am-2am; T Fenway)

Island Creek Oyster Bar

SEAFOOD $$$

4 🍴 MAP P128, C1

Island Creek claims to unite farmer, chef and diner in one space – and what a space it is. It serves up the region's finest oysters, along with other local seafood, in an ethereal new-age setting. The specialty – lobster-roe noodles topped with braised short ribs and grilled lobster – lives up to the hype. (📞617-532-5300; www.islandcreekoysterbar.com; 500 Commonwealth Ave; oysters $3, mains lunch $13-21, dinner $24-36; 🕐4-11pm Mon-Fri, 11:30am-11:30pm Sat, 10:30am-11pm Sun; T Kenmore)

Drinking

Bleacher Bar

SPORTS BAR

5 🍺 MAP P128, C1

Tucked under the bleachers at Fenway Park, this classy bar offers a view onto center field. It's not the best place to watch the game as it gets packed, but it's a fun way to experience America's oldest ballpark, even when the Sox are not playing.

If you want a seat in front of the window, get your name on the waiting list an hour or two before game time; once seated, diners have 45 minutes in the hot seat. (📞617-262-2424; www.bleacher-barboston.com; 82a Lansdowne St; 🕐11am-1am Sun-Wed, to 2am Thu-Sat; T Kenmore)

Cheeky Monkey Brewing

BREWERY

6 🍺 MAP P128, C1

A big brewing and drinking complex with plenty of potential. The service and food are variable, but the space is sweet and everybody loves the beer, which includes a couple of different IPAs, a stout, a fruity wheat beer, and other seasonal choices. Besides the Cheeky Monkey brews, there are pool and ping-pong tables and shuffleboard courts. (📞617-859-0030; www.cheekymonkeyboston.com; 3 Lansdowne St; 🕐5pm-2am Mon-Fri, from noon Sat & Sun; 🛜; T Kenmore)

Pavement Coffeehouse

CAFE

7 🍺 MAP P128, E1

Exposed brick walls hung with art create a bohemian atmosphere at this coffee lovers' dream. Berklee students and other creative types congregate for fair-trade coffee, bagel sandwiches, including many veg-friendly options (such as vegan cream cheese). (📞617-236-1500; www.pavementcoffeehouse.com; 1096 Boylston St; 🕐7am-8pm; 🛜; T Hynes)

Lansdowne Pub

IRISH PUB

8 ⊙ MAP P128, C1

Disclaimer: this place gets packed with college kids on weekends and on game nights. If you can stand the happy, sweaty people, it's a great vibe, especially if the Sox are winning. But if you're not into baseball, maybe you'll like the trivia (Wednesday), live-band karaoke (Thursday) or cover band dance parties (Friday and Saturday). (☏617-247-1222; www.lansdownepubboston.com; 9 Lansdowne St; cover $5; ⏱4pm-2am Mon-Fri, from 10am Sat & Sun; ⊤Kenmore)

Entertainment

Boston Symphony Orchestra

CLASSICAL MUSIC

9 ✪ MAP P128, F3

Flawless acoustics match the ambitious programs of the world-renowned Boston Symphony Orchestra. From September to April, the BSO performs in the beautiful Symphony Hall, featuring an ornamental high-relief ceiling and attracting a well-dressed crowd. (BSO; ☏617-266-1200, 617-266-1492; www.bso.org; 301 Massachusetts Ave; tickets $30-145; ⊤Symphony)

Huntington Theatre Company

THEATER

10 ✪ MAP P128, F3

Boston's leading theater company, the award-winning Huntington specializes in developing new plays, staging many shows before they're transferred to Broadway (several of which have won Tony Awards). (Boston University Theatre; ☏617-266-7900; www.huntingtontheatre.org; 264 Huntington Ave; ⊤Symphony)

House of Blues

LIVE MUSIC

11 ✪ MAP P128, C1

This legendary place was originally founded by Dan Aykroyd and Isaac Tigrett in a historic house in Harvard Square. Now the slick Fenway venue is bigger and better than ever (well, bigger), attracting national acts and some indie bands. (☏888-693-2583; www.hob.com/boston; 15 Lansdowne St; ⊤Kenmore)

Explore ⊚

Cambridge

Stretched out along the north shore of the Charles River, Cambridge is a separate city with two distinguished universities, a host of historic sites, and artistic and cultural attractions galore. The streets around Harvard Square are home to restaurants, bars and clubs that rival their counterparts across the river.

Short List

○ **Harvard Square (p138)** *Browsing the bookstores, rifling through the records and trying on vintage clothing.*

○ **Minuteman Bikeway (p144)** *Cycling from urban Cambridge to idyllic Bedford on this car-free bike trail.*

○ **Harvard Art Museums (p142)** *Checking out the varied collections and superb architecture.*

○ **Massachusetts Institute of Technology (p136)** *Discovering the fantastic, eclectic collection of public art.*

○ **Mt Auburn Cemetery (p142)** *Strolling around in search of famous gravestones, impressive artwork and elusive birds.*

Getting There & Around

Ⓜ Take the red line to Harvard station for Harvard Square, Central station for Central Sq and Kendall/MIT for Kendall Sq.

Neighborhood Map on p140

Harvard Square (p138) F11PHOTO/SHUTTERSTOCK ©

Top Experience 📷
Step Back in Time in Harvard Yard

Harvard was founded in 1836 and is America's oldest college. While the university now occupies vast areas in Cambridge, Allston and further afield, its geographic and historic heart remains at Harvard Yard. This is where red-brick buildings and leaf-covered lawns exude academia and where graduates proudly receive their degrees.

◎ MAP P140, F3

Harvard University

🝙 Harvard

Massachusetts Hall & Harvard Hall

Flanking Johnston Gate are the two oldest buildings on campus. South of the gate, **Massachusetts Hall** (1720) houses the offices of the President of the University. It is the oldest building at Harvard and one of the oldest academic buildings in the country. North is **Harvard Hall** (1766), which originally housed the library.

John Harvard Statue

The focal point of the yard is the **John Harvard Statue**, where every Harvard hopeful has a photo taken (and touches the statue's shiny shoe for good luck). Daniel Chester French's sculpture, inscribed 'John Harvard, Founder of Harvard College, 1638,' is known as the 'statue of three lies': it does not actually depict Harvard (since no image of him exists), but a random student; John Harvard was not the founder of the college, but its first benefactor in 1638; and the college was actually founded two years earlier in 1636. The Harvard symbol hardly lives up to the university's motto, *Veritas*, or 'truth.'

Widener Library

Behind this mass of Corinthian columns and steep stairs are more than 5 miles of books. Widener Library was built in memory of rare-book collector Harry Elkins Widener, who perished on the *Titanic*. Apparently Harry gave up his seat in a lifeboat to retrieve his favorite book from his stateroom. The library is not open to the public.

Memorial Hall

North of Harvard Yard, just outside Bradstreet Gates and across the Plaza, this massive Victorian Gothic building was built to honor Harvard's Civil War heroes. The impressive Memorial Transept is usually open for visitors to admire the stained-glass windows and stenciled walls. Most of the building's artistic treasures are contained in Annenburg Hall (not open to the public).

★ Top Tips

o Free campus tours from the Harvard University Information Center, inside the Smith Campus Center (p139).

o To go it alone, pick up a self-guided tour booklet (available in nine languages from the Smith Campus Center) or download an audio file or mobile app from the website.

o Finish your tour by climbing the steps of Robinson Hall for a perfectly framed photo of Memorial Hall.

✕ Take a Break

Harvard Square is packed with places to eat and drink, including several spots in the Smith Campus Center. You can't go wrong at Mr Bartley's Burger Cottage (p143).

Top Experience 📷
Savor the Science at MIT

The Massachusetts Institute of Technology (MIT) offers a completely novel perspective on Cambridge academia: proudly nerdy, but not quite as tweedy as Harvard. A recent frenzy of building has resulted in some architecturally intriguing structures. Also noteworthy: a fantastic collection of public art and a couple of unusual museums.

◉ MAP P140, B5

☑ 617-253-1000

www.mit.edu

77 Massachusetts Ave

🕐 info session incl campus tour 10am & 2:30pm Mon-Fri

Ⓣ Kendall/MIT

MIT Museum

Leave it to the brainiacs at MIT to come up with the city's quirkiest museum – the **MIT Museum** (617-253-5927; http://mitmuseum.mit.edu; 265 Massachusetts Ave; adult/child $10/5; 10am-6pm Jul & Aug, to 5pm Sep-Jun; P; Central). Exhibits explore questions about art, technology and everything in between, focusing on subjects as diverse as robotics, holograms, model ships and interactive sculpture. Expect great things from the MIT Museum in the coming years, as it is due to move into a larger facility in Kendall Square in 2021.

List Visual Arts Center

Small but subversive, the **List Visual Arts Center** (617-253-4680; http://listart.mit.edu; 20 Ames St, Weisner Bldg; donation $5; noon-6pm Tue, Wed & Fri-Sun, to 8pm Thu; Kendall/MIT) is a venue for art in its broadest forms, staging exhibits that ask probing questions about culture, society and science. This is also where you can pick up a map of MIT's magnificent collection of public art, including pieces by Alexander Calder, Sol LeWit and Henry Moore scattered around campus.

Stata Center

Of all the eye-catching buildings on the MIT campus, none has received more attention than the **Stata Center** (CSAIL; 617-253-5851; www.csail.mit.edu; 32 Vassar St; Kendall/MIT). The avant-garde edifice was designed by architectural legend Frank Gehry.

★ Top Tips

o Campus tours depart from MIT Information Center at 10am and 2:30pm, Monday to Friday.

o Student guides lead tours of the public art and the gallery exhibitions. Contact the List Visual Arts Center for more information.

o Visit the IHTFP Hack Gallery (http://hacks.mit.edu) to see MIT students' best pranks.

✕ Take a Break

When Barack Obama was in town he ate at **Area Four** (500 Technology Sq; pizza $18-28; 11:30am-10pm Mon-Fri, 10:30am-10pm Sat & Sun, cafe from 7am daily;), a popular pizzeria and coffee bar.

How about a grilled-cheese sandwich for lunch? **Roxy's Grilled Cheese** (292 Massachusetts Ave; sandwiches $5-9; 11am-11pm Sun-Thu, to midnight Fri & Sat;) specializes in the classic sandwich.

Walking Tour 🥾

Offbeat Harvard Square

Harvard Square is overflowing with cafes, book-stores, record shops and street musicians. Although many Cantabrigians rightly complain that the area has lost its edge, Harvard Square still has a thriving counterculture, if you know where to look. This route takes in some of the square's offbeat spots, both old and new.

Walk Facts

Start Raven Used Books;
T Harvard

Finish Harvard Book Store;
T Harvard

Length 1 mile; 30 minutes

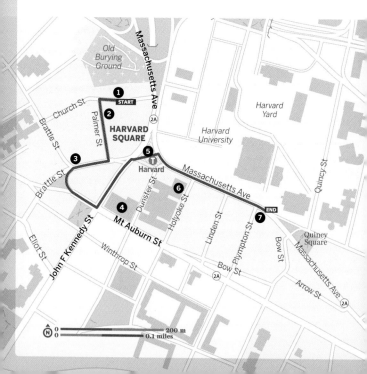

❶ Raven Used Books

Beloved by scholars, dilettantes and anyone who likes to browse, this **used-bookshop** (www.ravencambridge.com; 23 Church St; ⏰10am-9pm Mon-Sat, 11am-8pm Sun) is a trove of nonfiction treasures, especially on history, art and culture.

❷ Club Passim

Back in the day, Club 47 hosted the likes of Joan Baez, Bob Dylan and Joni Mitchell on its storied stage. Now known as **Club Passim** (p144), the basement joint still hosts top folk music acts.

❸ Brattle Square

Close to the historic **Brattle Theatre** (p145), this intersection is a main stage for street performers. Tracy Chapman played here in the 1980s and Amanda Palmer busked as a living statue in the 1990s. Puppeteer Igor Fokin performed here until his unexpected death in 1996. Look for the tiny memorial sculpture erected to honor him – and by extension, all street performers.

❹ The Garage

You can feel the grit at this parking garage turned **mini-mall** (36 John F Kennedy St; ⏰10am-10pm Mon-Sat, 11am to 8pm Sun). Some of the shops change frequently but a few long-standing institutions – especially Newbury Comics and Chameleon Tattoo & Body Piercing – attract a steady stream of goths, punks and other loyal shoppers.

❺ The Pit

In the center of Harvard Square, **Out of Town News** (⏰6am-10pm Sun-Thu, to 11pm Fri & Sat) has been selling newspapers and magazines from around the world since 1955. The sunken area nearby, aka 'the Pit,' is a popular spot for street artists, skateboarders and counter-culture youth to congregate.

❻ Smith Campus Center

The plaza in front of the **Smith Campus Center** (30 Dunster St; ⏰7am-midnight Sun-Fri, to 1am Sat) has hosted an ongoing chess tournament for 30 years and counting – look for the 'Play the Chessmaster' sign. It's also a top spot to take in the buskers, beggars and other Harvard Square goings-on.

❼ Harvard Book Store

The **Harvard Book Store** (p145) is not just a bookstore, but a reading community. Come in to browse the stacks and check out discounted 'seconds' in the basement. Next door, **Grolier Poetry Bookshop** (www.grolierpoetrybookshop.org; 6 Plympton St; ⏰11am-7pm Tue & Wed, to 6pm Thu-Sat) is a one of the country's most esteemed poetry bookstores.

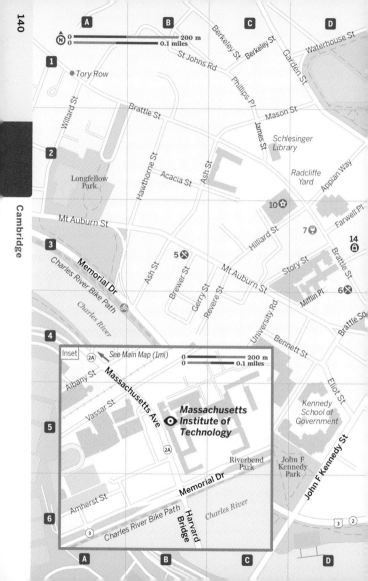

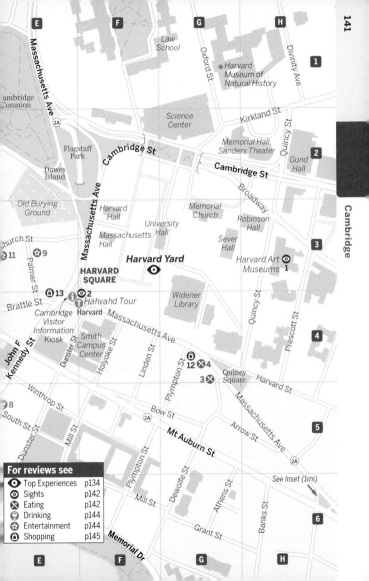

Cambridge

E
F
G
H

Massachusetts Ave

Law School

Oxford St

Divinity Ave

Harvard Museum of Natural History

1

ambridge Common

(2A)

Science Center

Kirkland St

Quincy St

Flagstaff Park

Cambridge St

Memorial Hall, Sanders Theater

Gund Hall

2

Dawes Island

Cambridge St

Broadway

Old Burying Ground

Massachusetts Ave

Harvard Hall

Memorial Church

Robinson Hall

Church St

University Hall

Sever Hall

3

⊙11   ⊙9

Massachusetts Hall

Harvard Art Museums ⊙1

Palmer St

Harvard Yard ⊙

HARVARD SQUARE

Quincy St

🔒13 ℹ️⊙2

Brattle St   Hahvahd Tour

Widener Library

Prescott St

4

Cambridge Visitor Information Kiosk   Harvard

John F Kennedy St

Smith Campus Center

Massachusetts Ave

Dunster St

Holyoke St

Linden St

Plympton St

🔒12 ⊗4
3⊗

Quincy Square

Harvard St

Massachusetts Ave

5

⊙8

Winthrop St

Bow St

(2A)

South St

Dunster St

Mill St

Mt Auburn St

Arrow St

(2A)

Plympton St

Dewolfe St

See Inset (1mi)

6

Mill St

Athens St

Grant St

Banks St

Memorial Dr

E
F
G
H

Sights

Harvard Art Museums
MUSEUM

1 MAP P140, H3

The 2014 renovation and expansion of Harvard's art museums allowed the university's massive 250,000-piece collection to come together under one very stylish roof, designed by architect extraordinaire Renzo Piano. The artwork spans the globe, with separate collections devoted to Asian and Islamic cultures, northern European and Germanic cultures and other Western art, especially European modernism. (617-495-9400; www.harvardartmuseums.org; 32 Quincy St; adult/child/student $15/free/free; 10am-5pm; Harvard)

Hahvahd Tour
WALKING

2 MAP P140, F4

This company was founded by a couple of Harvard students who shared the inside scoop on history and student life at the university. Now the company offers a whole menu of Boston tours, but the funny, offbeat Hahvahd Tour is the trademark. Tour guides are students who are not afraid to ask for tips. (Trademark Tours; 855-455-8747; www.harvardtour.com; adult/child $12/10.50; Harvard)

Eating

Hokkaido Ramen Santouka
JAPANESE $

3 MAP P140, G4

This worldwide chain is bringing a bit of Japanese simplicity and subtlety to Harvard Square. Service is pleasant and fast, while the noodles are perfectly satisfying. If you're wondering why the staff occasionally shout out, they are greeting and sending off their guests. (617-945-1460; www.santouka.co.jp/en; 1 Bow St; mains $11-17; 11am-9:30pm Mon-Thu, to 10:30pm Fri & Sat, to 9pm Sun; Harvard)

Brattle Street

West out of Harvard Square, Brattle St is lined with mansions that were once home to royal sympathizers, earning the nickname **Tory Row** (Map p140, A1). Nowadays, it's a pleasant place for a stroll to admire the gracious homes and glean some history from the environs.

At the end of Brattle St, **Mt Auburn Cemetery** (617-547-7105; www.mountauburn.org; 580 Mt Auburn St; 8am-8pm May-Sep, to 5pm Oct-Apr; 71, 73, Harvard) is worth the 30-minute walk west from Harvard Square. Developed in 1831, it was the first 'garden cemetery' in the US. Maps pinpoint the rare botanical specimens and notable burial plots. For more guidance, rent an audio tour at the gatehouse or download the Mt Auburn app.

Mr Bartley's Burger Cottage

BURGERS $

4  MAP P140, G4

Packed with small tables and hungry college students, this burger joint has been a Harvard Square institution for more than 50 years. Bartley's offers two dozen different burgers, including topical newcomers with names like Trump Tower and Tom Brady Triumphant; sweet-potato fries, onion rings, thick frappés and raspberry-lime rickeys complete the classic American meal. Be aware that this place is old school: credit cards are not accepted and there is no bathroom on site. (📞617-354-6559; www.mrbartley.com; 1246 Massachusetts Ave; burgers $14-21; ⏰11am-9pm Tue-Sat; Ⓣ Harvard)

Darwin's Ltd

SANDWICHES $

5  MAP P140, B3

Punky staff serve fat sandwiches, fresh soup and salads, and delicious coffee and pastries, all with a generous helping of attitude. The limited seating is often occupied by students who are in for the long haul (thanks to wi-fi access). So unless you need to get online, take your lunch to enjoy at JFK Park or Radcliffe Yard. (📞617-354-5233; www.darwinsltd.com; 148 Mt Auburn St; sandwiches

Mt Auburn Cemetery

ANGUS OBORN/LONELY PLANET ©

$9-12; ⏰6:30am-8pm Mon-Sat, from 7:30am Sun; 📶🚼; Ⓣ Harvard)

Alden & Harlow

AMERICAN $$$

6  MAP P140, D3

This subterranean space is offering a fresh take on American cooking. The small plates are made for sharing, so everyone in your party gets to sample the goodness. It's no secret that the 'Secret Burger' is amazing. Reservations are recommended. (📞617-864-2100; www.aldenharlow.com; 40 Brattle St; small plates $15-18; ⏰10:30am-2pm Sat & Sun, 5pm-midnight Sun-Wed, to 1am Thu-Sat; 🚼; Ⓣ Harvard)

Best Bike Trails 🚲

The **Charles River Bike Path** (Map p140; Storrow Dr & Memorial Dr; 🚲; T Harvard, Kendall/MIT, Charles/MGH, Science Park) is a popular cycling circuit runs along both sides of the Charles River between the Museum of Science and Watertown center. The round trip is 17 miles, but 10 bridges in between offer ample opportunities to shorten the trip.

Minuteman Bikeway (www.minutemanbikeway.org; T Alewife, Davis), the best of Boston's bicycle trails, starts near Alewife station and leads 5 miles to historic Lexington Center, then traverses an additional 4 miles of idyllic scenery and terminates in the rural suburb of Bedford.

Drinking

LA Burdick   CAFE

7 🚇 MAP P140, D3

This boutique chocolatier doubles as a cafe, usually packed full of happy patrons drinking hot cocoa. Whether you choose dark or milk, it's sure to be some of the best chocolate you'll drink in your lifetime. There are only a handful of tables, so it's hard to score a seat when temperatures are chilly. (617-491-4340; www.burdickchocolate.com; 52 Brattle St; 8am-9pm Sun-Wed, to 10pm Thu-Sat; T Harvard)

Shays Pub & Wine Bar   PUB

8 🚇 MAP P140, E5

A charming basement-level bar, Shays is an enduring favorite among Harvard students – definitely more 'pub' and less 'wine bar.' Inside, it's an intimate space that's often crammed with friendly folks noshing on excellent burgers and appetizers. Out front is a small brick patio full of sun-seekers jockeying for a table and watching the sidewalk goings-on. (617-864-9161; www.shayspubwinebar.com; 58 John F Kennedy St; 11am-1am Mon-Sat, noon-1am Sun; T Harvard)

Entertainment

Club Passim   LIVE MUSIC

9 ⭐ MAP P140, E3

The legendary Club Passim is a holdout from the days when folk music was a staple in Cambridge (and around the country). The club continues to book top-notch acts, single-handedly sustaining the city's folk scene. The colorful, intimate room is hidden off a side street in Harvard Sq, just as it has been since 1969. (617-492-7679; www.clubpassim.org; 47 Palmer St; tickets $10-32; T Harvard)

American Repertory Theater   PERFORMING ARTS

10 ⭐ MAP P140, C3

There isn't a bad seat in the house at the Loeb Drama Theater, where the prestigious ART stages new plays and experimental interpretations of classics. Artistic Director Diane Paulus encourages a broad interpretation of 'theater,' staging interactive murder mysteries, readings of novels in their entirety and robot operas. (ART; ☑617-547-8300; www.americanrepertorytheater.org; 64 Brattle St; tickets from $45; Ⓣ Harvard)

Brattle Theatre   CINEMA

The Brattle (see 7 Ⓜ Map p140, D3) is a film lover's *cinema paradiso*. Film noir, independent films and series that celebrate directors or periods are shown regularly in this renovated 1890 repertory theater. (☑617-876-6837; www.brattlefilm.org; 40 Brattle St; Ⓣ Harvard)

Sinclair   LIVE MUSIC

11 ⭐ MAP P140, E3

First-rate small venue to hear live music. The acoustics are excellent and the mezzanine level allows you to escape the crowds on the floor. The club attracts a good range of local and regional bands and DJs. (☑617-547-5200; www.sinclaircambridge.com; 52 Church St; tickets $15-35; ☺5pm-1am Mon-Wed, 5pm-2am Thu & Fri, 11am-2am Sat, 11am-1am Sun; Ⓣ Harvard)

Shopping

Harvard Book Store   BOOKS

12 🔒 MAP P140, G4

Family-owned and operated since 1932, the Harvard Book Store is not officially affiliated with Harvard University, but it is the university community's favorite place to come to browse. While the shop maintains an academic focus, there is plenty of fiction for less lofty reading, as well as used books and bargain books in the basement. (☑617-661-1515; www.harvard.com; 1256 Massachusetts Ave; ☺9am-11pm Mon-Sat, 10am-10pm Sun; Ⓣ Harvard)

Cardullo's Gourmet Shoppe   FOOD & DRINKS

13 🔒 MAP P140, E4

The excellent selection of New England products is a good source of souvenirs. Take home some Cranberry Bog Frogs (candy) from Cape Cod, maple sugar candy from Vermont and even clam chowder from Maine. (☑617-491-8888; www.cardullos.com; 6 Brattle St; ☺9am-9pm Mon-Sat, 10am-7pm Sun; Ⓣ Harvard)

Cambridge Artists Cooperative   ARTS & CRAFTS

14 🔒 MAP P140, D3

Owned and operated by Cambridge artists, this two-level gallery displays an ever-changing exhibit of their work. The pieces are crafty: handmade jewelry, woven scarves, leather products and pottery. The craftspeople double as sales staff, so you may get to meet the creative force behind your souvenir. (☑617-868-4434; www.cambridgeartistscoop.com; 59a Church St; ☺10am-6pm Mon-Wed & Sat, 10am-7pm Wed & Thu, noon-6pm Sun; Ⓣ Harvard)

Survival Guide

Long Wharf and downtown Boston (p75) ROMAN BABAKIN/SHUTTERSTOCK ©

Before You Go

Book Your Stay

o Boston offers a wide range of accommodations, from inviting guesthouses in historic quarters to swanky hotels with all amenities.

o Many stately homes that have been converted into B&Bs, offering an intimate atmosphere and personal service.

o Surprisingly few accommodations targeting budget travelers and backpackers.

Useful Websites

o **Lonely Planet** (lonelyplanet.com/usa/boston/hotels) Reviews and bookings.

o **B&B Agency of Boston** (www.boston-bnbagency.com) Fully furnished vacation rentals.

o **Bed & Breakfast Associates Bay Colony** (www.bnbboston.com) Huge database of un-hosted, furnished rooms and apartments.

o **Inn Boston Reservations** (www.innboston

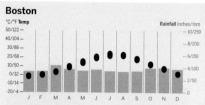

When to Go

o **Spring** Lovely weather and many events, especially at local universities.

o **Summer** Also busy, but hot and humid.

o **Autumn** Cool crisp weather and colorful fall foliage.

o **Winter** Temperatures and prices drop significantly.

reservations.com) Studio and apartment rentals in Boston's best neighborhoods.

o **Boston Green Tourism** (www.bostongreentourism.org) Up-to-date listings of ecofriendly hotels.

o **Boston Luxury Hotels** (www.bostonluxuryhotels.com) Individualized service for upscale travelers.

Best Budget

o **HI-Boston** (www.bostonhostel.org) A sparkling facility in the heart of Chinatown.

o **Bertram Inn** (www.bertraminn.com) Charming Brookline B&B.

o **Revolution Hotel** (www.therevolutionhotel.com) A cool creative budget option.

Best Midrange

o **Gryphon House** (www.innboston.com) A luxurious brownstone in Fenway.

o **Harding House** (www.harding-house.com) Homey haven in Cambridge.

o **Taylor House** (www.taylorhouse.com) A gracious Victorian in Jamaica Plain.

o **College Club** (www.thecollegeclubofboston.com) Cozy quarters in the Back Bay.

• **Newbury Guest House** (www.newbury guesthouse.com) Sweet retreat on Newbury St.

Best Top End

• **Liberty Hotel** (www.libertyhotel.com) Riverside luxury in a former jailhouse.

• **Verb Hotel** (www.theverbhotel.com) Verb is all about the vibe.

• **No 284** (www.no284.com) A boutique sleep in an opulent Back Bay brownstone.

Arriving in Boston

Logan International Airport

• Silver line bus (free) to South Station, then transfer to the T (subway).

• Blue line subway ($2.25 to $2.75) to central Boston; free shuttle from airport to Airport T station.

• Water shuttle ($9.25 to $15) Boston waterfront; free shuttle from airport to ferry dock.

• Taxi $25 to $30.

TF Green Airport

• Located one hour south of Boston in Providence, Rhode Island.

• MBTA commuter rail to Back Bay or South Station ($12, 90 minutes, 10 daily).

Manchester Airport

• Located 90 minutes north of Boston in New Hampshire.

• Flight Line Inc (www.flightlineinc.com) offers a shuttle service between MHT and Boston for about $140.

Getting Around

Bicycle

• Boston's bike-share program is **Blue Bikes** (www.bluebikes.com).

• There are 200 Blue Bikes stations around Boston, Cambridge, Brookline and Somerville, stocked with 1800 bikes that are available for short-term loan.

• Download the app or visit any bicycle kiosk to purchase your pass.

Pay $2.50 per half-hour or purchase a one-day Adventure Pass.

Boat

• The MBTA runs the F4 ferry – also known as the **Inner Harbor Ferry** (Map p34, E3; www.mbta.com; one-way $3.50; ⏰6:30am-8:25pm Mon-Fri, 10am-6:25pm Sat & Sun) – between Long Wharf and Charlestown Navy Yard.

• **Boston Harbor Cruises** (www.boston harborcruises.com) offers seasonal ferry service from Long Wharf to Boston Harbor Islands.

• **Boston Harbor Cruises Water Taxi** (www.bostonharborcruises.com/watertaxi) makes runs from Long Wharf to the airport and other waterfront destinations.

Bus

• The MBTA operates bus routes within the city, with schedules are posted on the website and at some bus stops along the routes.

• The standard bus fare is $2, or $1.70 with a Charlie Card. If you're transferring from the T on a Charlie Card, the bus fare is free.

o The silver line, a so-called 'rapid' bus, services the airport (SL1). The fare is $2.75 ($2.25 with a Charlie Card).

Subway (the T)

o The MBTA operates the USA's oldest subway, built in 1897 and known locally as the 'T'.

o There are four lines – red, blue, green and orange – that radiate from the principal downtown stations.

o Buy a paper fare card ($2.75 per ride) at any station or a Charlie Card ($2.25 per ride) at designated stations.

o Tourist passes with unlimited travel (on subway, bus or water shuttle) are available for periods of one day ($12) or one week ($21.25).

o The T operates from about 5:30am to 12:30am; schedules vary by line and station.

Taxi

o Cabs are plentiful but expensive. Rates are determined by the meter, which calculates miles.

o Expect to pay about $15 to $20 between most tourist points

within the city limits, without much traffic.

Essential Information

Accessible Travel

Boston attempts to cater to residents and visitors with disabilities by providing cut curbs, accessible restrooms and ramps on public buildings; but old streets, sidewalks and buildings mean that facilities are not always up to snuff. Download Lonely Planet's free Accessible Travel guides from http://lptravel.to/AccessibleTravel.

Sights Most major museums are accessible to wheelchairs, while the Isabella Stewart Gardner Museum, the Museum of Fine Arts and the Museum of Science offer special programs and tours for travelers with disabilities.

Activities Many tours use vehicles that are wheelchair accessible, including Boston Duck Tours and New England Aquarium Whale Watch. Walking tours such as

the Freedom Trail and the student tour of Harvard Yard are also accessible.

Transportation MBTA buses and commuter trains are accessible, although not all subway trains and stations are. See MBTA Accessibility (www.mbta.com/accessibility) for more information. Ferries to the Boston Harbor Islands, Provincetown and Salem are all accessible.

COVID-19 Requirements

o See www.boston.gov for the latest information about the 'B Together' vaccine mandate and the city's indoor mask policy.

o Get up-to-date information about US COVID-19 travel requirements at www.travel.state.gov.

Discount Cards

Thanks to its student-heavy population, Boston offers student discounts on admission to most attractions, so bring your ID. See www.smartdestinations.com and www.citypass.com

for various sights and activities passes that offer savings.

Electricity

Type A
120V/60Hz

Type B
120V/60Hz

Emergencies

For ambulance, fire or police, dial ☎ 911.

LGBTIQ+ Travelers

Out and active gay communities are visible all around Boston, especially in the South End and Jamaica Plain.

There is no shortage of entertainment options catering to LGBTIQ+ travelers. From drag shows to dyke nights, this sexually diverse community has something for everybody.

The biggest event of the year for the Boston gay and lesbian community is June's **Boston Pride** (www.bostonpride. org). At time of publication it was unclear if the 2022 event would be going ahead and no details are available for following years.

Bay Windows (www. baywindows.com) is a weekly newspaper for LGBTIQ+ readers.

Edge Boston (www. edgeboston.com) is the local branch of the national network of publications offering news and entertainment for LGBTIQ+ readers.

Money

ATMs widely available. Credit cards accepted at most hotels, restaurants and shops.

ATMs

ATMs are great for quick cash, but watch out for ATM surcharges. Most banks in Boston charge at least $2.50 per withdrawal. Look for ATMs outside banks and in many shops, crocery stores and gas stations.

Credit Cards

Major credit cards are accepted at hotels, restaurants, gas stations, shops and car-rental agencies. In fact, you'll find it hard to perform certain transactions, such as renting cars or purchasing concert tickets, without one.

Tipping

Members of the service industry depend on tips to earn a living – tips constitute their wages.

Baggage carriers $1 to $2 per bag.

Bar & restaurant staff 20% for good service,

15% for adequate service; less than 15% indicates dissatisfaction with the service.

Housekeeping $3 to $5 for one or two nights, more for longer stays.

Taxi drivers 10% to 15% of the fare.

Public Holidays

New Year's Day January 1

Martin Luther King Jr's Birthday Third Monday in January

Washington's Birthday Third Monday in February

Evacuation Day March 17

Patriots' Day Third Monday in April

Memorial Day Last Monday in May

Bunker Hill Day June 17

Independence Day July 4

Labor Day First Monday in September

Columbus Day Second Monday in October

Veterans Day November 11

Thanksgiving Day Fourth Thursday in November

Christmas Day December 25

Safe Travel

Boston is a relatively safe city and most tourists are unlikely to be targets of crime.

Crime rates are higher in outlying Boston neighborhoods.

Reports of harassment of people of color are more common in Boston than other Northeastern cities.

Telephone

All US phone numbers consist of a three-digit area code followed by a seven-digit local number. Even if you are calling locally, you must dial all 10 digits. If you are calling long distance, dial 1 plus the area code plus the seven-digit number.

Area Codes

○ Boston ☎617

○ Suburban Boston ☎781

○ North Shore ☎978

○ South Shore ☎508

○ Country code ☎1 for USA

○ International dialing **code** ☎011

Toilets

○ Travelers will usually find clean bathrooms in museums, large hotels, restaurants, shopping malls and large stores.

○ For public bathrooms, visit fire stations and libraries.

○ The self-cleaning 'City Toilet' (which costs 25¢ to use) is found at key spots around town.

○ The city has an interactive map of public bathrooms (www.boston. gov/departments/311/ public-restrooms-city-boston).

Tourist Information

Boston Common Information Kiosk (p61) provides maps and all kinds of tourist information; starting point for the Freedom Trail and many other walking tours.

The **Greater Boston Convention & Visitors Bureau** (www. bostonusa.com) website is packed with traveler's information.

Boston Harbor Islands Pavilion (p89) will tell you everything you need to know to plan your visit to the Boston Harbor Islands.

Cambridge Visitor Information Kiosk (Map p140, E4; ☎617-441-2884; www.cambridge-usa.org; Harvard Sq; ⏰9am-5pm Mon-Fri, to 1pm Sat & Sun; Ⓣ Harvard) has detailed information on current Cambridge happenings.

Massachusetts Office of Travel & Tourism (www. massvacation.com) has information about events and activities throughout the state.

National Park Service Visitors Center (p82) has loads of information about the Freedom Trail sights. There is an additional NPS Visitors Center at the Charlestown Navy Yard (p36).

Visas

○ The US has a Visa Waiver Program in which citizens of certain countries may enter the US for stays of 90 days or less without first obtaining a US visa.

○ For an up-to-date list of countries included in the program, see the US Department of State website (www.travel. state.gov).

○ Under the program you must have a round-trip ticket (or onward ticket) that is nonrefundable in the US and you will not be allowed to extend your stay beyond 90 days.

○ To participate in the Visa Waiver Program, travelers are required to have a passport that is machine readable. Also, your passport should be valid for at least six months longer than your intended stay.

○ Travel under the Visa Waiver Program requires pre-approval under the Electronic System for Travel Authorization (ESTA) at least three days before arrival. There is a $14 fee for processing and authorization (payable online). Once approved, the registration is valid for two years.

○ Travelers entering by land do not need to file an ESTA application.

○ Those who do need a visa should apply at the US consulate in their home country.

Responsible Travel

Leave a Light Footprint

○ Travel around the city on foot, by public transportation or on **Blue Bikes** (p149).

○ Carry a tote bag to reduce use of plastic and avoid the 5-cent surcharge for store bags.

○ Don't forget your reusable water bottle.

Support Local

○ Support local farms and artisanal food producers at the **Boston Public Market** (p84).

Educate Yourself

○ Learn about green energy at the Catching the Wind exhibit at the **Museum of Science** (p50).

○ Explore the impact of climate change on our oceans at the Blue Planet Action Center in the **New England Aquarium** (p83).

○ Check out the green roof at the **Boston Children's Museum** (p82).

Behind the Scenes

Send Us Your Feedback

We love to hear from travelers – your comments help make our books better. We read every word, and we guarantee that your feedback goes straight to the authors. Visit **lonelyplanet.com/contact** to submit your updates and suggestions.

Note: We may edit, reproduce and incorporate your comments in Lonely Planet products such as guidebooks, websites and digital products, so let us know if you don't want your comments reproduced or your name acknowledged. For a copy of our privacy policy visit lonelyplanet.com/legal.

Mara's Thanks

To the poet-for-hire on the Boston Common: thanks for reminding me that there is a poem for every season and every reason. At times, it's a complicated or even nonsensical poem, and forget about rhyming, but still...a poem.

Acknowledgements

Cover photograph: Boston Tea Party Ships (p80), Dominionart/ Shutterstock ©
Back cover photograph: George Washington statue, Boston Public Garden (p64), Jorge Salcedo/ Shutterstock ©
Photographs pp28–9 (left to right): f11photo, Co Leong, Sean Pavone/ Shutterstock ©

This Book

This 5th edition of Lonely Planet's *Pocket Boston* guidebook was researched and written by Mara Vorhees. The previous edition was written by Gregor Clark. This guidebook was produced by the following:

Destination Editor
Trisha Ping

Senior Product Editors
Kirsten Rawlings, Martine Power, Victoria Smith

Cartographers Rachel Imeson, Alison Lyall

Product Editors Damian Kemp, Ross Taylor

Book Designers
Norma Brewer, Brooke Giacomin

Assisting Editors
Katie Connolly, Samantha Cook, Mani Ramaswamy, Monica Woods

Cover Researcher
Gwen Cotter

Thanks to
Ronan Abayawickrema, Kate Ellison, Evan Godt, Ashley Gow, Sonia Kapoor, Linda McLaurin, Susan Paterson, Saralinda Turner, Will Turton, Gavin Whenman

Index

See also separate subindexes for:

⊗ **Eating p157**
⊜ **Drinking p158**
✪ **Entertainment p158**
⌂ **Shopping p158**

Index

Our Writer

Mara Vorhees

Mara writes about food, travel and family fun around the world. Her work has been published by BBC Travel, *Boston Globe, Delta Sky, Vancouver Sun* and more. For Lonely Planet, she regularly writes about destinations in Central America and Eastern Europe, as well as New England, where she lives. She often travels with her twin boys in tow, earning her an expertise in family travel. Follow their adventures and misadventures at www.havetwinswilltravel.com.

Published by Lonely Planet Global Limited
CRN 554153
5th edition – Jul 2022
ISBN 978 1 78868 394 4
© Lonely Planet 2022   Photographs © as indicated 2022
10 9 8 7 6 5 4 3 2 1
Printed in Malaysia